Apart from being the founder and editor of NewsBiscuit, John O'Farrell is the author of such bestselling books as *An Utterly Impartial History of Britain*, *The Best a Man Can Get*, *This Is Your Life*, *May Contain Nuts*, and *Things Can Only Get Better* as well as three collections of his popular *Guardian* column. An award-winning comedy scriptwriter for such shows as *Spitting Image*, *Smith and Jones* and the film *Chicken Run*, he now regularly appears on TV and radio, on programmes such as *Have I Got News for You*, *Newsnight Review* and *Grumpy Old Men*. His books have been translated into over twenty languages, although how the gags work in Norwegian is anyone's guess.

www.**rbooks**.co.uk

www.newsbiscuit.co.uk

Also by John O'Farrell

Non-fiction
An Utterly Impartial History of Britain
Things Can Only Get Better
Global Village Idiot
I Blame the Scapegoats
I Have a Bream

Fiction
The Best a Man Can Get
This Is Your Life
May Contain Nuts

JOHN O'FARRELL

ISLE OF WIGHT TO GET CEEFAX

AND OTHER GROUNDBREAKING STORIES FROM NEWSBISCUIT

TRANSWORLD PUBLISHERS
61-63 Uxbridge Road, London W5 5SA
A Random House Group Company
www.rbooks.co.uk

First published in Great Britain
 in 2008 by Doubleday
an imprint of Transworld Publishers

A CIP catalogue record for this book
is available from the British Library.

ISBN 9780385615358

Addresses for Random House Group Ltd companies outside the UK
can be found at: www.randomhouse.co.uk
The Random House Group Ltd Reg. No. 954009

The Random House Group Limited supports The Forest Stewardship
Council (FSC), the leading international forest-certification organization.
All our titles that are printed on Greenpeace-approved FSC-certified
paper carry the FSC logo.
Our paper procurement policy can be found at
www.rbooks.co.uk/environment

Typeset in Berling
Printed and bound in Great Britain by
Butler, Tanner & Dennis

2 4 6 8 10 9 7 5 3 1

JOHN O'FARRELL

ISLE OF WIGHT TO GET CEEFAX

AND OTHER GROUNDBREAKING STORIES FROM NEWSBISCUIT

Doubleday

LONDON · TORONTO · SYDNEY · AUCKLAND · JOHANNESBURG

ISLE OF WIGHT TV LAUNCHES
PIMP MY MOBILE LIBRARY

The Isle of Wight's domestic island TV channel has had a surprise hit with its new show *Pimp My Mobile Library*.

1 January

In the programme various librarians from the island compete to see who can soup up their mobile library before the vans speed around a village circuit dispensing Catherine Cookson novels to local pensioners.

With go-faster flames around the expanded wheel arches and fluorescent lights under the jacked-up chassis, the vans now cruise the island's hot spots at night, honking loudly at passing old ladies and burning rubber as the drivers attempt handbrake turns around the war memorial. 'Dem rides is like well sick, bro,' said librarian Edith Whiteside. 'If any ho touch my shaggin' wagon, I put a cap in their ass, innit.'

With the advent of the internet and multi-channel TVs, the island's library service had feared that their future might be in jeopardy. 'We had to modernize and diversify if we were going to survive,' said head librarian Marjorie Harrison. However, an inquiry is now under way as to whether it is appropriate for a mobile library that normally lends hardback romantic fiction and Mills & Boon to also sell crack cocaine, ecstasy and low-grade heroin.

MAN BREAKS NEW YEAR'S RESOLUTION BEFORE EVEN WAKING UP

2 January

A Bristol man set a new world record yesterday morning by breaking his New Year's resolution before he had even realized what year it was. Mike Palmersgate has set himself different targets every January for the last five years but sadly has never managed to keep to any of them. Last year he went jogging two days in a row before failing to get out of bed on the third day. Two years ago he promised himself he would give up smoking, but lasted until 4 January. But this year, his New Year's resolution was broken while Mike was still fast asleep.

From 1 January, Mike had promised his girlfriend Sharon that he would try to stop dressing up in her underwear. But at seven o'clock yesterday morning, Sharon heard movement in the bathroom and went to investigate. There she saw Mike prancing about in the fancy lingerie that he had bought her for Christmas.

'Mike was sleepwalking,' she explained. 'He's not a transvestite or anything, it was just another one of his bad dreams. He does this a lot, poor thing. But it's amazing that he managed to find the underwear hidden away in the back of my wardrobe, then get it all out of the packet and fiddle with all the straps and put on the stockings and everything.'

Mike's previous somnambulant antics have involved him taking money from Sharon's purse, sleepwalking all the way to ladies' clothes shops and buying bras and knickers. Another time he was fast asleep yet still walked to a drag bar having applied lipstick and mascara.

'I generally wake him very gently and explain that he's been sleepwalking again. Then he takes off the ladies' clothes and I take them back to the shop. I used to get cross with him wearing my dresses and everything, but you can hardly blame anyone for what they do in their sleep.'

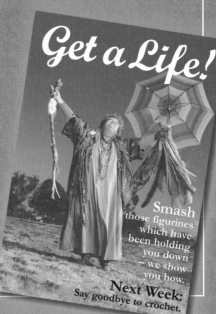

Teenagers on work experience banned from air-traffic control

5 January

Schoolchildren gaining practical experience of the workplace will no longer be permitted to manage the traffic at busy airports, following a number of recent safety concerns.

At the age of fourteen or fifteen, most Year 10 pupils are seconded to a local business or retail outlet to gain practical experience of office life before making further education or career choices. However, a number of pupils who did their work experience at Heathrow Airport have been judged to be insufficiently attentive or mature to be left in charge of busy air-traffic lanes.

Fifteen-year-old Gary Emmett from Hayes Technical College spent a week on the computers at Heathrow. 'You had to get these little planes on the screen on to this, like, narrow strip? It's not as good as Grand Theft Auto, cos you only get one life.' Another Hayes pupil was sent home after he made two planes on the screen bump into one another 'to see what would happen'. 'The acoustics on these computers is, like, amazing,' said Johnny Finch, 14. 'I got them to crash on the screen but it sounded like the big explosion was right outside the window!'

'They were only supposed to be making the coffee and doing a bit of photocopying,' said Bill Hendry, the headteacher who organized the Heathrow work-experience allocations. 'Unfortunately a small minority of irresponsible pupils thought it would be amusing to get out of doing PE for the rest of term by crashing a jumbo jet into the school gymnasium.'

However, the pupils deny that they were to blame for crashing any planes. 'How could I?' said Gary. 'I wasn't even on the air-traffic programme most of the time. Whenever I got bored I just switched the computer to MSN and chatted to my friends who were supposed to be working at the international currency markets.'

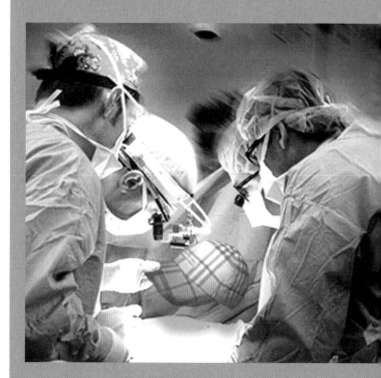

SURGEONS PERFECT 'CLASS-CHANGE' OPERATION

7 January

Private health practices using the latest surgical techniques have successfully carried out the first operation allowing the patients to permanently alter their social class.

Building on decades of experience from surgeons who have changed people's appearance or even their gender, medical teams are now able to assist people who feel they were born into the wrong level of society.

After months of counselling, Reg Smith of east London decided to alter his identity. 'Well, I'd always felt that I was born into the wrong class,' said Reg before his op. 'Like, when we'd have our tea break on the building site I used to secretly drink lapsang souchong, and, come Saturday, I'd tell the lads I was off to the greyhounds, whereas in fact I was dressing up in cravats and browsing through antique shops in Richmond.' Reg's procedure involved a twelve-hour operation, with the surgeon removing the naked lady tattoo on his arm, sewing up the crack in his bottom, making his front teeth stick out and wrinkling his nose up into a permanent superior sneer. Reginald Smythe, as he will now be known, affected not to know the interviewer after the operation, and instructed her to contact his staff if she wished to make an appointment to speak to him.

Another person considering a class-change operation was Patricia Dickens: 'I always pretended I was working class, you know, wore jumpers with holes in the arms, lived in a squat in Hackney, that sort of thing. But it was only skin deep really – I mean my father was still Sir Gerald Dickens of Dickens and Jones.' Patricia later postponed a permanent change when she read the consent form explaining that she would have to live in a tower block with four kids and a Rottweiler, and she wouldn't be allowed to go home to Sussex at the weekends.

But critics say the procedure is unethical, and that in some cases the operation can go tragically wrong. After Reginald Smythe's class-change operation, friends say that they 'don't know whether he is a chav or a toff'. 'He drinks decaffeinated cappuccino, but with five sugars.' Reg is stuck with a bizarre accent, which swings wildly between upper class and cockney, meaning that the only job open to him is becoming an alternative comedian. Mr Smythe has stated that he intends to pursue the class-change scandal through the proper legal channels, 'and then smash their bloody face in'.

US TELLS SUICIDE BOMBERS 'THOSE 72 VIRGINS ARE ALL GUYS'

9 January

THE WAR ON TERROR TOOK A NEW TURN TODAY WITH THE LAUNCH OF A BOLD NEW PROPAGANDA CAMPAIGN AIMED AT PREVENTING ANY MORE SUICIDE BOMBERS IN IRAQ OR ELSEWHERE IN THE MIDDLE EAST.

US intelligence has distributed leaflets in Arabic stating that owing to the high demands that have been placed on Paradise by so many Islamic martyrs, the powers that be have had to widen the definition of 'virgin'.

The belief that martyrs who die in the holy war will be rewarded in Paradise with seventy-two virgins is thought to have persuaded many young Muslim militants to lay down their lives in terrorist attacks. The US military maintains that this promise has given the Jihadists an unbeatable edge when it comes to recruiting sexually frustrated young men. 'But when the Koran said "virgins", they never specified whether they were chicks or guys,' said a US source in Iraq. 'What we are saying is that with so many martyrs arriving in Paradise, the babes all got taken ages ago. Basically today if you choose to be a suicide bomber it means you want to do bum sex with guys. And, like, seventy-two of them, so you must be a pretty committed homo; that's not like just trying it once when you were drunk in the school dorm . . . '

Leaflets have been dropped over suspected al-Qaeda training camps, explaining that anyone who decides to be a suicide bomber must be a great big gay. It is illustrated with a cartoon of a suicide bomber wearing sticks of dynamite strapped to his chest, which match his big black motorcycle helmet and leather trousers. The suicide bomber is saying, 'Do you think these explosives make my bum look big?'

US Intelligence denies that the so-called 'al-Queerda Initiative' represents a desperate last throw from a military leadership that has run out of ideas, and remain convinced that this tactic could mark the turning point against the insurgents. But they are also in talks with American church leaders about making Christian heaven a little more appealing. 'What red-blooded US soldier is gonna risk going to heaven just to stand around on a cloud wearing a white frock and strumming a harp? That sounds kinda gay too.'

Apple unveil iNvisible iBook

11 January

Apple's Steve Jobs stunned reporters at an Apple product launch yesterday by apparently holding nothing but air in his hands.

An excited Jobs explained: 'The iNvisible iBook is the lightest, slimmest, most beautiful Apple product yet. Almost invisible to all but the coolest, smartest consumers, this takes the appreciation of design and technology to a new level.'

At this point many of the assembled journalists and technology correspondents squinted and then suddenly gasped in admiration at the beauty and design of the new Apple product, agreeing that it was definitely worth the $2,999 price tag. 'Anyone with any taste or appreciation of computer design can see that this is the best product on the market.'

When one reporter asked what exactly the iNvisible iBook could do, Jobs simply replied, 'See for yourself!' and the reporters gasped at the many varied functions of the machine and the speed with which it accomplished them. The only blip in the presentation was a slight disturbance at the back of the hall when a small boy shouted out, 'There's nothing in his hand!' but he was quickly removed by security.

In a later statement Jobs explained that the boy had been a long way back and had poor vision, hence his inability to see the new iNvisible iBook. For his second media appearance of the day, Jobs was wearing Apple's new super-cool range of clothing to go with the iNvisible iBook.

Middle-class couple concerned about sponsored child's academic progress

12 January

A Manchester couple have expressed concern about the educational progress being made by the child they sponsor in Uganda and are threatening to pull her out of her village school. Doug and Emily O'Sullivan from Wilmslow say they are now seriously worried about the future prospects of 'Beatrice', from the village of Buteyongera in Central Uganda, following a New Year's update from the charity WorldVision, which they claim revealed only a mediocre academic performance.

'The report we received from the charity asserted that Beatrice and her family are doing well with their little farm, and in her photo she looks happy enough, but frankly I'm a little alarmed by a rating of "satisfactory" for her schoolwork,' said Doug. 'I think you'll agree not many students make it to Oxbridge by being "satisfactory".'

Emily O'Sullivan agreed with

her husband's assessment, insisting that seven-year-old Beatrice is exceptionally bright and should be on the village school's Gifted and Talented register. When Emily called WorldVision about this they were unable to confirm whether such a list even existed and admitted that there was no top set for Maths or English since Beatrice is only given basic schooling with forty other local children in a makeshift classroom next to her village's only surviving tree.

The O'Sullivans sent Beatrice educational DVDs and CD-ROMs intended to boost academic performance, but were disappointed that the school had not made more use of them. 'Something about there being "no computers or electricity" or something – frankly the culture of excuses is partly what is holding back the most able pupils like Beatrice.'

The O'Sullivans are now threatening to take their sponsored child out of school and send her to a more rigorous selective private school in the Ugandan capital. 'It's a two-hour walk there and back every day, but it's worth it if the school is at the top of the local league tables,' said Doug. 'Her father may have to sell his livestock to pay the fees, but you can't put a price on a child having the opportunity to learn the cello.'

GAZA BORDER CROSSING TO GET TESCO METRO

The British supermarket giant is opening one of its popular Tesco Metro stores on the breached border point between the Gaza Strip and Egypt.

14 January

The mini-supermarkets have proved popular in British urban areas, where commuters have been able to get themselves basic foodstuffs on the way home from work. Now busy Gazan Palestinians will be able to pop out for a pint of milk and a ready meal for one before returning to their bombed-out, besieged enclave, which remains without power or reliable running water. 'Our ready-washed Caesar salads are a great favourite,' said store manager Gill Summerby, 'and we are pushing the WeightWatchers range for those refugees who need to lose a few pounds!'

Thousands of Palestinians have already poured into the Sinai Peninsular to get the ready-washed Caesar salads, the gravadlax medley and Tesco's popular range of organic quiches. 'It took a while to get the special offers right,' said Ms Summerby. 'Not knowing much about the complex religious and ethnic divisions in this corner of the Middle East, we just put up a big sign saying "Guaranteed Kosher". It turns out that the Gaza Strip is not full of Israelis despite what it seemed to show on the old atlas in our office. But I'm sure our "Every Little Helps" message will strike a chord in the disputed territories.'

An Israeli military deputation has already been to the store to make sure the Gaza Tesco Metro was not selling Kalashnikovs or mortar launchers, and left with a pint of milk, a small sliced loaf and an 'Aromatic Crispy Duck for Two'.

Unlike with most Tesco developments, existing local businesses have not complained yet that they'll be put out of business, as they haven't got anything to sell anyway. However, Ms Summerby still detected a great deal of anger among her customers from the war-torn Palestinian enclave. 'I understand their anger, but we can't supply only free-range chicken at this stage. They are just going to have to be patient.'

Printer ink tops $1,000 a barrel

18 January

The grim economic picture darkened further today with news that the price of ink for printer cartridges has reached an all-time high of a thousand dollars a barrel on the New York futures exchange.

The world's most traded commodity has seen a steady rise in price over recent months due to supply problems, increased demand from China and a failure of consumers to send their empty cartridges to the charity recycling centre and just leaving them in their desk drawer instead.

So dependent is the global economy on printer ink that there are concerns the United States may take military action against crude-ink producers in the Middle East unless the situation improves. 'You know what the invasion of Iraq was really about, don't you?' said Spike Harris of the Stop the War Coalition. 'Printer ink, yeah! PresidINK Bush is in the pay of the big ink companies, and the whole lot of 'em have got blood on their hands. And black ink obviously.'

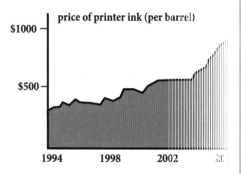

price of printer ink (per barrel)

$1000

$500

1994   1998   2002

19 January

Kennel Club recognized breeds to include werewolf

The British Kennel Club has raised eyebrows in the dog-showing world after announcing that the werewolf is finally going to be recognized as an official dog breed, following years of campaigning from devoted werewolf lovers.

The large powerful wolf-like breed will compete at this year's Crufts in the 'Utility' section, alongside such traditional family favourites as the Dalmatian, the schnauzer and the French bulldog. Ben Fogle, a long-standing supporter of the controversial werewolf breed, declared himself delighted with the decision: 'Werewolves have long suffered from a poor reputation based on exaggerated tabloid reports of them savaging lone humans during the full moon, leaving people to join the "undead" until the bloodline is broken. In fact they are just being friendly, but people don't know how to react to them.'

The police, however, have expressed concern that lycanthropes may now become a status pet for the likes of drug-dealers, gang leaders and Princess Anne. Werewolves were not among the proscribed breeds listed in the Dangerous Dogs Act, but fans of the breed admit that this official recognition may make the werewolf popular with those who do not have the time to train this 'exuberant' breed properly. 'People get a werewolf puppy, not thinking about how big they get when the moon is full and the blood lust must be sated,' said Ben Fogle. 'But it is not fair to blame the dog if the pavement is littered with human ribs and internal organs. It's up to the owners to clear up after their pet. Blame the owner, not the werewolf!'

An investigation is under way after it was discovered that town planners and architects in the Midlands are playing a massive game of Scrabble by constructing letter-shaped buildings to spell out words that can then be identified on Google Earth.

Two years ago, a new office and shopping complex in Dudley was praised for its creative use of new materials on a challenging elongated site, where it 'defined a new relationship between the built environment and external spaces'. But what nobody realized was that when viewed on Google Earth, the building actually spelt out 'HADDOCK'. The challenge was then on for a rival architect, who had been commissioned to design a site directly to the south of this one, to incorporate the second 'D' from the middle of the word. His team-mates in the local planning department soon gave permission for a new residential development, without revealing that they had successfully spelt out 'DHAL' with massive fifty-metre letters that had become the homes for hundreds of people.

On being challenged that 'you can't have curry dishes as they are not proper English words', the office responsible explained that 'dhal' was in fact in the *Oxford English Dictionary*, and was 'a type of tropical woody herb much cultivated in the tropics'. The large L-shaped building at the southernmost point of the development necessitated the demolition of a rural school, thereby earning them a triple word score.

Town planners playing Scrabble using Google Earth

20 January

It has emerged that after a successful challenge last year, that 'you couldn't have "THERMOS" because it was actually a proper noun', a new hospital and old people's care home were demolished as the architects and planners were forced to take their go again.

The officers in Dudley's town-planning department who based their decisions on this game of Google Earth Scrabble have now been sacked, but not before they had given the green light to a new City Academy that joined up to the last letter of HADDOCK and used up their last letters: U, F and C.

Google

Environmentalists to withdraw protection for 'rubbish animals'

23 January

The World Wide Fund for Nature has decided that certain species of animal are facing extinction owing to their own crappy design, and unless they are prepared to evolve a bit quicker, then their imminent extinction will be nobody's fault but theirs.

The ruling has been ratified by other environmental groups around the world who are fed up with trying to preserve fussy eaters or rare mammals that refuse to learn not to walk trustingly up to fat South Africans who are carrying great big hunting rifles.

'There is a rare flightless bird in Tasmania called the Ewonda,' said WWF spokesman Michael Deane. 'It is an elusive and beautiful bird. However, as birds go, the whole

"flightless" thing is a bit of a basic design fault. Since man brought cats to the island, this shy nocturnal creature has been hunted almost to extinction. People say the cats shouldn't be there. We say: "Learn to fly, 'bird'."'

The conference passed the resolution overwhelmingly and then broke for a buffet lunch of wind-dried panda with a white rhino jus.

Thousands of celebrities audition for *America's Next Top Accountant*

25 January

Top singers, actors, dancers and rock stars have all been queuing up in the hope of getting a steady job in accountancy in the latest talent show to top the ratings in the United States.

'I always had this secret dream that I might one day work in some area of financial management. This TV show means that at last there is the chance that my dreams might come true . . . ' said an excited Beyoncé as she practised with her calculator and spreadsheet. Contestants have just thirty seconds to impress the judges with their advice on tax returns and deductible expenses. But only a few lucky ones will go forward to 'Accountancy Camp' where the heartache and elation of discovering who has the talent to go all the way will be watched by millions of viewers.

'Ever since I was a kid I used to practise accountancy in my bedroom,' confessed Amy Winehouse. 'I've sent a few tables of some projected expenses into all the big firms, but even though they kept rejecting me, I always believed I had the financial acumen and auditing skills to make my dreams come true.'

'This means the whole world to me,' wept Rihanna after being told that she wouldn't be going forward to the next round. The judges have been accused of being too brutal with some of the accountancy hopefuls. 'You call that deductible!' shouted one of the professionals to a tearful Madonna as he tore up her illegible receipts from some holiday gift shop. 'Forget it, sweetheart. You'll never make an accountant; you'll just be an iconic rock superstar for the rest of your life.'

'I'll come back next year, and the year after that,' sobbed Madonna. 'I'll just keep hold of my dream until I reach the top. As long as I can offset the projected expenses against my partner's small business on an overseas leaseback account . . . No, hang on, that's not right . . . '

Archbishop of Canterbury converts to Islam

27 January

Dr Rowan Williams has failed to quell the row over his recent comments with the announcement that he has been fully accepted into the Muslim faith. He claims to see no inconsistency with his new religion and his continuing role as the leader of the Anglican faith.

'Both religions are saying basically the same thing,' said Rahman Muhammad bin Williams, as he now wishes to be known, 'and I hope to bring together two aspects of these two major world faiths. So we will still have the Church of England Christingle Jumble Sale. But instead of getting a jar of home-made jam in the raffle, the winner gets to drive a car bomb into the American Embassy.'

Dr Williams has said that it is important for England's established church to reflect the cultural and religious diversity within today's Britain. This point was reiterated by the Rastafarian Bishop of Durham, who was later arrested when police became suspicious about the contents of his incense-burner.

Dr Williams dismissed the latest controversy as he headed off to buy a glittery tissue-box holder for the back of his car. 'Let us not forget that as Archbishop of Canterbury I am not head of the Church of England. That privilege remains with the Defender of the Faith, Her Majesty the Queen. Or Shariz el-Izbeth as she now wishes to be known.'

BOND VILLAIN'S UNDERGROUND MISSILE SILO 'DID NOT HAVE PLANNING PERMISSION'

<u>30 January</u>

The criminal mastermind and arch-enemy of British secret agent James Bond has found himself in trouble with his local council after it was discovered that his secret underground missile base was built without the required permission from his local planning office.

Ernst Blofeld, owner of a number of large properties on the Isle of Wight, has spent millions of dollars on the nerve centre from which he was planning to hold the entire world to ransom. His plans hit an unexpected hitch last Tuesday, however, when he was contacted by the planning department, who'd become aware that his massive underground control centre and nuclear launch pad had never come before the island's planning-control committee.

'Even though it is mostly underground, it still exceeds the permitted development for this type of property,' explained Councillor Rosalind Johnson (Con). 'We understand that the old mansion divides into two as the missile launchers rise up out of the ground from where they can fire enough nuclear weapons to destroy all the major cities of Western Europe and the American East Coast. If this were the case then we would want to ensure that the missile launchers are in keeping with the traditional late-Victorian style of this Grade II listed building within a conservation area.'

Under the Isle of Wight's strict planning laws Ernst Blofeld may be left with no choice but to demolish the epicentre of his evil empire. The criminal genius has said he will appeal to the council, stressing the number of jobs that his secret lair would provide for the local economy. 'I will be looking for any nuclear-rocket scientists living in the Ryde area, a couple of hundred henchmen proficient in martial arts, and maybe a big bloke with metal teeth or a robotic arm or something . . .'

In fact dozens of armed guards were already on site when the planning officer delivered the official notification from the council, but found themselves insufficiently trained for this type of crisis. 'We weren't quite sure how to react,' said one. 'We were expecting James Bond to parachute into the silo, take us all on, then use some gadget to blow it all up. Instead we have been defeated by some 55-year-old bureaucrat with a form from the council. It's very disappointing.'

Councillor Johnson added, 'Actually there is no way James Bond would have gained the required permission to parachute into a built-up area. It's against Health and Safety.'

Fight after snooker champions 'never put no coins on table'

1 February

There were ugly scenes at the World Snooker Championships this weekend when the final between Mark Selby and John Higgins was interrupted by other competitors claiming they were next on the table.

Indicating a couple of pound coins that they had left on the side, the defeated semi-finalists Sean Murphy and Stephen Maguire told the finalists that they had no right to be playing as they 'never put down no money'. Famed snooker referee Jan Verhaas attempted to calm the situation between them, only to be struck across the head with a cue while a Scottish voice cried, 'Stay out of it, mate, you ain't even fucking playing.'

The atmosphere was already tense after Murphy had repeatedly left his pint on the side of the table, and shouted 'In the hole!' just as the finalists took every shot. A debate ensued over whether they had to nominate a hole for the black and Mark Selby had to keep saying, 'Scuse me, mate, you're dropping ash on the felt.' But no one had expected a full-scale pub brawl to kick off which then spilt out into the car park, where Stephen Maguire was knocked into a pile of plastic crates, while commentator Dennis Taylor, now in tears, shouted, 'Leave it, Mark, he's not worth it.' A snooker ball was smacked against Maguire's nose, causing a severe nosebleed, at which point the referee picked up the ball and carefully placed it back on its correct spot on the table.

All four have been barred from the venue and the final will resume today with a couple of thirteen-year-olds who just like rolling the balls down the table and watching them bouncing off the cushion.

SCIENTISTS DEVELOP CONDOM-FLAVOURED FRUIT

2 February

A team of British scientists have developed a range of condom-flavoured fruits in an attempt to improve the diet of 'sex-addicted British teenagers'. Research shows that teenagers dislike the unfamiliar taste of fresh fruit and vegetables; the hope is that they may be tempted to try them if they come in more familiar flavours.

The Cambridge-based researchers first isolated the chemical flavour agents of several leading-name condoms, including Trojan and Durex. Then, using a complicated technique, they managed to splice the condom molecules with the DNA of a selection of popular fruits, producing the distinctive nose-wrinkling bitter flavour of a fresh condom. The fruit will soon be available in three varieties: Featherlite Banana, Ribbed Strawberry and French Tickler Tangerine, which comes with a spermicide topping.

'This isn't just some amusing novelty product,' explained Professor Andrew Pryor, who led the innovative project. 'If we can get some vitamins into these kids we have a real chance of improving their lives and future prospects. We are hoping that condom-flavoured bananas will soon feature as one of their five portions of fruit or vegetable a day.' But he warned that further progress on this project will be painstakingly slow. 'Splicing the DNA is not so hard,' he said, 'it is opening the condom packet that takes the time.'

Makers of Action Man sued for inadequate equipment

6 February

Action Man maker Hasbro is to be sued for failing to provide adequate equipment for toy soldiers going into battle. A support group representing the plastic fighting dolls is claiming that Action Men have been put at risk by being sent into battle with faulty or unsuitable military hardware. A spokesman for the group told reporters: 'It's an international disgrace that can only be called penny-pinching. Plastic boots, guns that don't fire and "armoured" cars that afford no protection against being knocked off the sofa with a giant plastic sword – our boys deserve better.'

But Hasbro has defended its record, issuing a statement saying, 'Spending on equipment for Action Man has increased by fifteen per cent in real terms in recent years, and we refute all allegations that our soldiers have been sent into battle with anything less than the very best in toy weaponry.'

One Action Man, who asked to remain anonymous, claimed, 'My plastic boots were a nightmare to get on and off from day one. In the end one of the boots came off with my foot still inside it.' Another reported problems with his Eagle Eyes, which left him permanently looking left. This resulted in a disadvantageous battle situation against a large plastic dinosaur and some small plastic cowboys on the difficult terrain of the living-room carpet. 'Our boys should never have had to go into battle with trousers that had lost their popper at the back,' said one military expert. 'They never stood a chance against that giant real-life kitten.'

GOVERNMENT SLAMMED FOR 'SNOWMAN SKILLS SHORTAGE'

7 February

This week's blast of cold weather has revealed a desperate shortage of snowman-making skills in Britain's young people, claimed a damning survey yesterday.

With widespread school closures following the winter's first heavy fall of snow, there were expectations that a major display of high-quality snowmen would suddenly appear in the country's parks and playgrounds.

Visitors to Britain were shocked, however, to see that national snowman standards had plummeted since the last cold winter, with the worst display of snow sculptures ever recorded. 'Your country's snowmen are bullshit,' said French Canadian Jean-Pierre Bertillon. 'You are just making big lumps of slush with clichéd features that look nothing like human beings.' Another tourist said it was pathetic to see the country of great sculptors like Henry Moore and Barbara Hepworth producing such dismal attempts at the human form. Journalists from around the world have relished reporting Britain's national humiliation with English snowmen being laughed at by newsreaders as the joke item at the end of their evening bulletin.

In a packed House of Commons, the Conservative education spokesman blasted the government for removing snow skills from the national curriculum and failing to promote 'winter crafts' as a specialism in the government's flagship City Academies.

'But I don't accept that there are no high-quality snowmen in Britain today,' said the Prime Minister. 'I have seen dozens of brilliant, original and realistic snowmen made by British children this week.' The Prime Minister neglected to add the detail that these snowmen had all been created digitally on Nintendo Sim-Snow '07.

ESSEX MAN COMPLETES ALL THE PORN ON THE INTERNET

9 February

Wayne Harris, an unemployed builder from Chigwell, made history this week by becoming the first man in the world to have perused all of the pornography on the internet.

The historic moment occurred late on Thursday 8 February, when Mr Harris started to notice that some of the images he was accessing seemed a little familiar, and suddenly he realized he was now on his second time around.

'This is a great British success story,' said a spokesman for 10 Downing Street. 'When it comes to reaching the South Pole or circumnavigating the globe the British have too often been the runners-up. But here is an example of a twenty-first-century British explorer who has planted the Union flag on the new frontier of the digital age.'

Mr Harris, or 'Sir Wayne' as he is soon expected to become, never set out to achieve this historic first but admitted, 'I just really like looking at pornography. I spend most days, and nights in fact, just clicking from one link to the next, and entering random obscene ideas in my search engine. But I suppose that is dedication of a sort, and I feel a sort of pride that I should be the most porn-obsessed man in the whole world.'

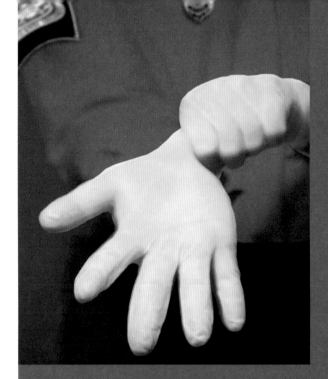

Wildean quip regretted as US Customs begin cavity search for genius

11 February

An English undergraduate was subjected to an extended internal body search yesterday for declaring to US Customs: 'I have nothing to declare except my genius.' Morris Stevens, a foppish Cambridge literature student, was immediately marched to a back room, where two burly customs officers pulled on rubber gloves and carried out an extended cavity search for the genius of which Morris had boasted.

'Third time this week and it don't get any funnier,' said Customs Officer Charlie Gill. 'Smart-ass English private-school boys who think they are Oscar Wilde. We have a procedure now. We say, "You couldn't resist it, could you?" And if they say "I can resist everything except temptation, officer," then we pin them to the floor.'

Gill also explained that some jokers are also asked what they think of the United States, and if they trot out the Oscar Wilde line that 'America is the only country that went from barbarism to decadence without civilization in between' then they get 300-pound 'Big Brad' to pull on the rubber gloves. 'Brad has much bigger fists. It's our own tribute to a different side of Oscar Wilde.'

Man dismayed as petrol station flowers fail to end relationship

14 February

Peter Wilson, a 29-year-old systems analyst from Solihull, was said to be 'upset and bewildered' after his Valentine gifts of a wilting bunch of carnations and a box of Maltesers from the local Esso garage were received with an enthusiastic hug and kiss from his long-term girlfriend Clare.

The last-minute present, which even had the price left on, was supposed to have been the final straw in a three-month campaign of obnoxiousness intended to make his girlfriend realize their relationship was

over and leave him. However, after she found the gifts on the sofa where he'd dumped them, Clare skipped to the kitchen to complete a romantic dinner, leaving Pete to write complaining texts about her attitude on the iPhone she'd got him to mark the occasion.

Yearning for the single life, but hoping to keep their rented flat, Peter went out of his way to be rude about her friends and showed up drunk and three hours late when her parents came to dinner. He 'forgot' their anniversary, a task made all the more difficult by the fact it was also her birthday and New Year's Eve. Yet through all this Clare remained upbeat and understanding, leaving Peter completely exasperated.

'I'm running out of options,' he complained, cutting his toenails and watching the women's beach volleyball on Sky Sports 3. 'For the past month I've been raising my eyebrows every time she has a biscuit and asking if she "really thinks she needs that?" but she won't take the hint. If this goes on much longer, I'm just going to have to tell her I've been sleeping with her sister.'

Heart transplant on Valentine's Day romantic, ultimately fatal

15 February

Doctors treating Barry Wilkins today described the failed heart-transplant surgery that took place on Valentine's Day and resulted in his death as 'really quite romantic'.

Mr Wilkins, who had a condition known as cardiac hypertrophy, had been waiting for a suitable donor for sixteen months when his girlfriend, Miranda Lewis, was involved in a fatal motorcycle accident on Monday. Soon after, doctors were delighted to discover that she was a genetic match. 'She literally gave him her heart,' said one visibly moved nurse. 'I wish my boyfriend would do that for me.'

Medical staff played Marvin Gaye and lit scented candles in the operating theatre to accentuate the romantic mood. Chief Surgeon Colin McKay said, 'It was a lovely Valentine's Day moment. There were roses everywhere and we all wore red scrubs, which also helped disguise the massive amounts of blood.'

Unfortunately, three hours into the operation Mr Wilkins suffered a 'gross haemorrhage and myocardial infarction', possibly caused by the essential oils interacting with the anaesthetic.

'Barry's death obviously put a damper on the mood,' said Mr McKay. 'My thoughts are with his family at this difficult and ironic time.'

AMAZONIAN INDIANS DELIGHTED WITH HARDWOOD GARDEN FURNITURE

Environmentalists were thrown on to the defensive yesterday when it emerged that garden benches, tables and chairs made from Amazonian hardwoods are incredibly popular with the very people whose homelands are being destroyed by illegal logging.

'Deforestation has destroyed the land of my ancestors,' said Xingu, an Amazonian tribesman from the remote Tumucumaque valley. 'I have nowhere to hunt, or to find wood for fire or shelter. But you have to admit, this colonial-style garden seat with matching drinks table is a bargain at just $44.50. I don't know how they do it at that price.'

Despite efforts to ban the trade in Amazonian hardwoods, many furniture manufacturers continue to use materials obtained from the diminishing rainforests. Environmental groups have attempted to organize boycotts against companies that still use protected Amazonian hardwoods. Greenpeace will be embarrassed that many of the threatened indigenous tribesmen of the Amazon are impressed with the quality and good value of the wooden furniture produced in defiance of their protected status.

'It makes me sort of proud,' said Xingu, 'to think that something as useful as this drop-leaf garden table came from wood logged here. Why couldn't my ancestors ever make anything as useful as this fully adjustable teak sun-lounger?'

When an area of rainforest has been cleared of trees it is often used for grazing cattle, with the resulting low-cost beef being used by global burger chains. 'So we can sit round our teak picnic table under the telescopic parasol and have a slap-up McDonald's meal for only $4.99,' said Xingu. 'Life doesn't get any better than this!'

Teachers' bureaucracy being copied off best friend in morning

Teachers under pressure to complete endless reports, tables and statistics are copying their answers off their friends on the way to school in the morning.

'Everyone does it,' says Ms Alex Cribley, a science teacher from north London. 'On the bus I sit next to my friend Ms Simpson, who is Head of Year at another school. I just copy my Self-Evaluation form off of her. Same with Fisher Family Trust stats and the English as an Additional Language and Special Educational Needs figures. I usually make one or two numbers slightly different so I don't get caught.'

Government funding based on all this data has been criticized for failing to hit the right areas of pupil need, but an unnamed source at the Department of Education said teachers weren't to blame for this. 'It's because the Education Minister just copied his regional allocations off the Minister for Health.'

Jeremy Clarkson launches 'Squashed Animal Watch'

18 February

Following the success of last A27M07 weekend's RSPB Birdwatch, motoring enthusiast Jeremy Clarkson has launched another nationwide nature survey – Squashed Animal Watch.

'We are asking people all over the country to spend one hour looking out for flattened road-kill and then just take five minutes to enter the results on the *Top Gear* website,' he announced.

Early statistical returns show high numbers for traditional British favourites: crushed hedgehogs, mangled grey squirrels and lots of perfectly preserved, completely flat frogs and toads.

However, there are concerns that some over-enthusiastic *Top Gear* fans are boosting their tally by going around deliberately running over small furry animals. A National Park warden from Dartmoor said, 'We have had reports of middle-aged men in mid-range sports cars, driving at speed towards rabbits, crows and a badger. One bloke actually took the trouble to reverse over a pygmy shrew. In a steamroller.'

But Clarkson defended the cars-versus-nature initiative. 'No doubt we'll get the usual whingeing from the politically correct bunny-huggers, but this is about the survival of the fittest. The hedgehog's natural predator is now the 4x4. So it's important that we have accurate statistics for how many animals are failing to get out of the way of British motorists. And then next year we can try and improve on that figure . . .'

Office manager 'pretty sure' he got away with new wig

ANDREW MULLINS, A PROPERTY MANAGER FOR BRENT COUNCIL IN LONDON, WAS RELIEVED TO REPORT THAT HIS FIRST DAY AT WORK SPORTING A NEWLY ACQUIRED TOUPEE HAD PASSED WITHOUT INCIDENT.

19 February

Forty-eight-year-old Mullins had taken the decision to buy a hairpiece after concluding that combing over the 'slightly thinning' hair on the top of his head with strands from the back and sides was taking too long in the mornings. He didn't expect anyone would really notice the change, but upon arriving at the office first thing on Monday Mullins had loudly announced to the staff that he had 'discovered a new barber', just in case.

The rest of the day passed relatively uneventfully for the property manager who, as he wandered the corridors of cubicles in his department, was pleased to hear the sound of furious typing of emails whenever he walked by. The afternoon was then spent leading a meeting on the proposed office team-building day where suggestions from his staff included wind-surfing, kite-flying, and 'one rather left-field suggestion of visiting a wind tunnel'. Yet he maintained that there are no bad ideas in brainstorming, and it wasn't long after that that the group collectively agreed on a crafts day, where they could all learn about rug-weaving, which, Mullins said, 'certainly makes a change from paintball'.

'They're a good bunch,' reflected the manager, affectionately known by his staff as Donald Trump ('because I'm in charge of all this property, obviously'), before commenting on another example of their kind and caring nature: 'Here, look at this, it's a sponsorship form that went around today. They're all selling syrup of figs to raise money for this charity that supports rodents that are being cruelly kept in horrible conditions. Those poor, poor hamsters . . . ' he said as he enjoyed a bowl of cereal his secretary had dropped in, because he looked like he might need some Shredded Wheat.

TRADITIONAL PIPES NOW OUTNUMBERED BY CRACK PIPES

20 February

The British statistical survey has thrown up a quirky piece of data that moralists and church groups have seized upon as a significant milestone in the continuing decay of modern British society.

For the first time there are now more people smoking crack pipes than traditional tobacco pipes, with almost no overlap between the two groups of users. 'Old-fashioned pipes are still popular with certain types of older bearded men; model railway enthusiasts, canal barge restorers and the like, but curiously these tend to be among the least likely people to head into the inner cities to score crack cocaine off their dealer,' reported the survey.

Ann Widdecombe MP declared that it was symptomatic of the political correctness of today's nanny state that so much effort had been put into stopping people from smoking tobacco, while drug use continued to rise. Taking a symbolic puff from an old-fashioned Meerschaum pipe, she declared, 'There, what is the harm in that? And yet, if I inhale from this ghastly modern crack-pipe thing . . . wow, that is good shit, man. I am fuckin' flyin', know what I mean?'

WINEHOUSE KEEN TO READ HER OWN BIOGRAPHY 'TO FIND OUT WHAT SHE'S BEEN UP TO'

21 February

A spokesman for Amy Winehouse has revealed that the singer is very excited about the recent biography and hopes to discover exactly what has happened during the last few years of her life.

Publishers of the controversial book by Nick Johnstone became nervous after the singer began bombarding them with requests for an advance copy. They presumed that the Grammy winner must be concerned about potentially libellous allegations, but in fact she was just curious to know how she came to wake up on the floor of a hotel bathroom with smudged mascara, a wonky beehive and a number of empty vodka bottles.

'Amy is hoping that the book might jog one or two memories,' said her manager down the phone. 'Her short-term memory is not quite as strong as it might be,' he continued, before breaking off to say, 'I'm your manager, Amy . . . '

'She can vaguely recall walking into a recording studio in 2002, but after that it's all a bit of a blur. Amy is apparently worried that she might have possibly made a bit of an arse of herself on the odd night out,' he resumed. 'She's just grateful that at least there aren't any embarrassing photos out there.'

New car to be powered by anger

23 February

Car designers faced with the joint problems of increasing traffic and inner-city pollution have come up with a radical solution by developing a car powered entirely by the driver's anger.

Top Gear presenter Jeremy Clarkson was highly impressed by the power of the so-called AngerCar™ as he drove around the Wandsworth one-way system. 'I'm currently doing a comfortable thirty m.p.h. – oi, get out of the way you stupid bastard – no, forty m.p.h. – oh no, bloody speed cameras – fifty m.p.h. - road humps, God I hate those . . . '

The owners of AngerCars™ are encouraged to display annoyingly smug and self-righteous stickers in their back window to annoy other drivers and generate more fuel. Unfunny Garfield stickers or signs warning that the driver has 'Show Dogs in Transit' have also been shown to generate enough irritation to power the vehicles for hundreds of miles. 'Anger is the perfect fuel for modern drivers,' explained the Transport Minister, 'as it is cheap, clean and endlessly renewable – no, don't block the yellow box, you stupid tosser!' he shouted.

'Oh no, not that git . . . ' groaned the driver in the next lane.

Test drives in traffic-free rural areas, however, have proved unsatisfactory, as the AngerCar kept coming to a halt. This design fault is to be countered with a specially adapted personal Sat Nav, which tells you where you went wrong in your life, the tragic consequences of the mistakes you made, and how much you would now be earning if you hadn't been so stupid.

Dalai Lama failed to declare good karma in official register

2 March

Tenzin Gyatso, the exiled spiritual leader of the Tibetan people, found himself at the centre of a political controversy today when it was revealed that he had neglected to enter a number of gifts and good deeds done to him by fellow Buddhists in the official register.

Since the so-called Cash for Reincarnation Scandal of the late nineties, it has been mandatory that senior Buddhists report all gifts, considerate deeds or just kindly thoughts of which they have been the chief beneficiary.

'The karma register was devised to ensure that powerful Buddhists were not abusing their position, but it has got to the stage that you can't even hold a door open for the Prime Minster of Sri Lanka without him having to make a note of it,' claimed a spokesman for the Dalai Lama.

Among the specific charges against the spiritual leader of Tibet is that on 13 February he left his umbrella in a restaurant but was reunited with it when a fellow diner came rushing out after him having noticed his absent-mindedness. 'There is no record of this random act of kindness,' said the Official Karma Watchdog, 'nor of the occasion when His Holiness mentioned that he liked early Britpop, and one of his office support staff did him a compilation CD of Blur, Pulp and Oasis.'

A spokesman for the Dalai Lama claimed that this 'very minor scandal' had been whipped up by the Chinese authorities to try and deflect from their own oppression in Tibet, but added, 'Anyway, failing to register the good karma is bad karma, so the karma is cancelled out and he's back to where he was in the first place.'

ZOMBIE REGRETS FILLING OUT ORGAN-DONOR CARD

4 March

Clive Hill's return from the dead as a brain-eating zombie was slightly hampered last night after he discovered that several vital organs, including his corneas, were missing.

'I'm kicking myself, to be honest,' said Mr Hill. 'Being one of the walking undead is a challenge I'm willing to step up to. But being undead and blind takes me right out of the game. Thanks to the organ-donor register, I just can't keep up with other zombies.'

As several youths drank and joked at a local Luton cemetery, Mr Hill was supposed to rise menacingly from the earth and advance towards the screaming teenagers. 'Instead I staggered around blindly and fell right back into my grave again. They were screaming all right; they were screaming with laughter,' Mr Hill explained. 'It's probably on YouTube as we speak.'

Successive attempts to stagger threateningly towards unsuspecting young couples also failed miserably as Mr Hill kept bumping into trees and fences, and had to be taken by the arm by his intended victims who helpfully asked the bewildered zombie where he was trying to get to.

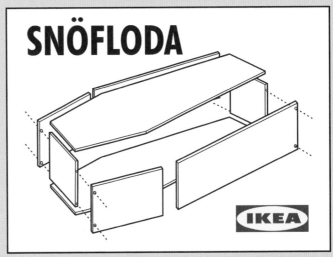

ANIMAL-RIGHTS ACTIVISTS RELEASE PANTOMIME HORSE INTO WILD

6 March

A pantomime horse that was performing at the Theatre Royal, Windsor, has been kidnapped by animal-rights extremists and released into the wild. 'Trigger', who was appearing nightly in *Snow White and the Seven Dwarfs*, was captured on Sunday night and, according to a statement by the Animal Liberation Front, 'is now running free somewhere in the English countryside'.

The ALF have consistently stated their opposition to animals being kept in captivity for performing purposes, but this is the first time they have released a fancy-dress animal. The would-be terrorists broke into the back of the historic theatre after the Wednesday matinée and led the unsuspecting animal into a waiting horsebox parked by the stage door.

'These animal-rights fascists have no understanding of pantomime horses,' said Trigger's distraught handler Jennifer Hartley-Smythe. 'Trigger loved his work here, nodding his head and doing the hokey-cokey on stage for the little children.'

Police have asked members of the public to look out for Trigger, who can be easily distinguished from other horses as he looks nothing like a horse. He is a large ungainly animal with big fluttering eyelashes and a smiley, toothy grin. 'Anyone encountering him should ask him to come back to Windsor,' said a spokesman for Thames Valley Police. 'If he stamps his hoof once, it means "yes", if he stamps his hoof twice, it means "no".'

UNOPENED WATNEY'S PARTY SEVEN DETONATED BY ARMY EXPERTS

8 March

Builders excavating foundations in south London were forced to clear the entire site when they discovered a Party Seven giant beer can that had remained unopened since the 1970s.

Nearby homes were also evacuated before army beer disposal experts were called in.

The Watney's Party Seven was a popular sight at domestic parties in the 1970s, and was traditionally opened by somebody hammering at the top with a screwdriver and rolling pin, usually knocking the giant can on to the floor a couple of times and denting it, before finally making a small hole in the top which would spray a fountain of weak fizzy beer on to the ceiling.

However, explosives experts believed that having remained buried under rubble and earth for thirty years, this unopened Party Seven might have become extremely volatile; perhaps capable of smashing windows, stunning family pets and spraying tasteless keg beer over a wide area.

Eventually the army called in a specially built robot, which attempted to carry out a controlled explosion by piercing the metal lid using a number of kitchen implements, including a barbeque skewer and a bread knife, before a hand drill was finally fetched from the garage. Once opened, the beer was drunk by two gatecrashers who one local claimed had still not gone home from the original party in 1973.

English football managers to import foreign adverbs

9 March

The Premier League is bracing itself for a new flood of overseas imports after FIFA agreed to the free transfer of foreign adverbs.

A football agent explained: 'There is a massive shortage of adverbs in the English game, as they all seem to go off to poncy sports like cricket and tennis. In football English words have always performed nice and bright and I think they done great up to now, even if it's been a big ask to play adjectives and nouns out of position.'

Newcastle assistant manager Ray Parkin, who has already welcomed a number of signings from Paris Saint-Germain, said, 'We have waited *nerveusement* to see how the new boys would fit in. At the start, when they was tackled from behind by a big English preposition they tended to react a bit *furioso*. However, once they got going they fitted in *bene* and played very *atemberaubend*, compared to the English lads who also done great. I mean done *buono*.

English players meanwhile are attempting to improve their grasp of continental languages. After a season of Italian lessons, many of them have already mastered the word *pizza*.

IRAQ 'SPLITTING ALONG ASTRO-LOGICAL LINES'

11 March

Hopes of an end to the violence in Iraq were looking remoter than ever this week as UN observers reported that insurgents were dividing according to the signs of the zodiac.

Traditional Shia and Sunni loyalties were being further complicated by an ongoing and increasingly bloody conflict between the Water, Fire and Earth signs.

Things have gone downhill ever since the execution of Saddam Hussein. As a Taurus, the former dictator came from a star sign that represented approximately one-twelfth of the Iraqi population, who now feel particularly resentful and persecuted, although they were slightly mollified to learn that friends may be important to them this weekend.

Corporal James Carter, whose unit is stationed just outside Basra, said the power struggle in the south is becoming increasingly bitter: 'There has been a running gun battle between the traditionally incompatible Piscean and Sagittarian forces. We had the UN guys in there trying to mediate, but the bloodshed seemed to be over whether tomorrow would be a good day to raise long-standing concerns about work issues or whether health matters could come to the fore by the weekend.'

Corporal Carter's men had come under gunfire from a Capricorn position to their rear, though with those born under the sign of the Goat being notoriously prone to putting things off, he was able to negotiate a temporary ceasefire 'until they felt ready to face new challenges'. Using an interpreter and a loudhailer, Corporal Carter guaranteed that local militia units would be allowed time to deal with romance issues that had been bubbling under, adding, 'And if it is your birthday today, you should follow your instincts over the coming year, start putting yourself first; this doesn't make you selfish. Be decisive, but take care.'

COURAGE AWARD FOR MAN WHO THREW OUT OLD COMPUTER CABLES

13 March

A Guildford man has been honoured in the People's Courage Awards for showing 'outstanding bravery and strength of character' in throwing out a number of old computer cables, even though he could not remember where they came from and could not be certain that one of them might not come in handy again at some point in the future.

John McHugh, 26, had apparently been complaining for some time that he was no longer able to close the bottom drawer of his home workstation, as it was so jam-packed with old power leads, redundant chargers, USB links, iPod speakers, power cables and modem cables, and the printer wire from an Amstrad 8256.

'We suggested stuffing the lot into a Tesco's bag and chucking it on top of the wardrobe,' said flatmate Bryan Whitesmith, 'or storing them all in the loft with the vague intention of maybe trying to flog them as a job lot on eBay one day. But none of us could have guessed for a moment what John was actually going to do.'

According to eyewitnesses, the normally cautious local librarian simply took the packed wooden drawer out of the workstation, walked out of the front door and tipped the entire contents into a wheelie bin. 'We were stunned,' said Whitesmith. 'There was a curly off-white cable with, like, a round five-pronged little plug on one end and a square blue plastic bit on the other. That must have been essential for something. And the redundant phone chargers might have worked as a back-up charger for another mobile phone that he might purchase in the future. It was madness.'

But when McHugh's courage came to the notice of the organizers of the People's Courage Awards, they knew there could only be one winner. 'We are fed up of giving out these awards to blokes who have rescued people from the sea, or kids that have kept smiling through terrible diseases,' said a spokesman. 'Chucking out mystery computer cables: that's what I call courage.'

McHugh said he was going to spend the prize money on computer peripherals, specifically connecting his universal card reader to his laptop, adding, 'I'm sure I used to have a cable for that somewhere.'

Minor Royals to be merged

Princess Michael of Kent and the Duchess of Kent may already be the same person

Sad Soho launches nostalgic 'porn experience'

15 March

Retired sex-industry workers who were driven out of Soho by a council clean-up are launching their own industrial heritage museum, so that tourists can remember what red-light districts were like in the days before people got their pornography off the internet.

Visitors to the 'Porn Experience' are given dirty raincoats as they arrive, then make their way through the displays of 1970s mags and sex aids by guides dressed as authentic sex workers. There are Danish sex mags featuring men with big moustaches and sideburns and original 'Randy Raquel' inflatable dolls with real hair and bright blue eyeliner. Well-thumbed copies of *Health and Efficiency* sit alongside sex films on easy-to-use Super 8 overhead projectors.

'Back in the 1970s, this part of London was nothing but strip clubs, private cinemas and hardcore sex shops,' muses Ronnie Diamond, founder of the Porn Experience. 'You'd hear the merry cry of the traditional prostitute: "ten bob for straight or a quid up the tradesman's!" On every corner there was a vicious-looking pimp and his wizened drug-addicted tarts with needle marks on their arms. Now look at it . . . ' sighs the former porn boss. 'Young couples meeting in cafés, people browsing round Waterstone's,

friends enjoying lunch in Pret a Manger. It breaks my heart to see it like this . . . '

Authenticity is key at the Porn Experience; as they arrive at the strip-club section punters enjoy what they think is a free glass of champagne, but are then presented with a bill for a hundred pounds. However, there is no pretending that business is as good as it was back in the old days. 'Visitor numbers just aren't what I had hoped,' Ronnie Diamond admits, 'even though the strip show employs some of the original prostitutes who worked here forty years ago . . . '

Problems were exacerbated for the heritage museum when a couple of ex-boxers from 'Gangster Guided Tours' turned up and smashed in the window, saying they were owed 'protection', before re-enacting the payment of hush-money to retired detectives narrating the passing 'Corrupt Police Heritage Walk'.

SCHOOL BANS CRUCIFIXIONS

16 March

A Catholic secondary school in south London has been forced to ban the crucifixion of disruptive pupils after the local authority ruled that the practice may offend the religious sensitivities of some non-Christian families.

St Mary's Sacred Heart School in Wandsworth has come under fire in the past for its extreme and old-fashioned Catholic ethos, which has previously seen pupils condemned to an eternity in hell for failing to reach a level 5C at the end of Key Stage 3. It is the practice of crucifying its students, however, that was highlighted as 'an area of some concern' during a recent Ofsted inspection.

'It's fine for children who come from ultra-Christian families where this sort of thing might be normal,' said Ken Charlton from the Education Authority. 'But since St Mary's Sacred Heart was forced to admit a proportion of non-Christians, the use of crucifixion as a form of punishment might be seen to be religiously inappropriate for, say, Hindus or Muslim pupils.'

The fundamentalist faith school is now being encouraged to use detentions and fixed-term exclusions as a deterrent to pupils who break school rules or the Ten Commandments. The exclusions may be for up to two weeks rather than the previous arrangement whereby children were cast out into the wilderness for forty days. Nor will Spanish oral tests be allowed to follow the 'Inquisition' model in future.

Headmistress Sister Anne-Marie Callaghan was angry at the bureaucratic infringement of the school's religious freedoms: 'First they said that schoolchildren couldn't wear a crucifix; next they say we're not allowed to nail kids to a cross and leave them out on the sports field. It's just political correctness gone mad.'

Yet there is one consolation for the school. Following the publicity surrounding the case, St Mary's has received a number of extra enquiries from parents keen to educate their children in the ultra-Christian faith environment, including applications from former Education Minister Ruth Kelly and the Blairs looking for somewhere to send young Leo.

Swimming pool introduces 'chatting lanes' for the elderly

18 March

Help the Aged has given a warm welcome to the decision by the management of St Albans Swimming Baths to set aside a special swimming lane purely for pensioners who want to stand in the middle of the pool and chat to each other.

Water Activities Co-ordinator Sarah Morrison said, 'We are simply responding to a growing demand by our most loyal customers. A lot of our older bathers don't really want to swim at all. They tend to come just for the social side. Now they don't need to feel self-conscious about sticking to water activities that suit them, such as gossiping, moaning about their husbands, complaining about the council, and laughing very loudly and slowly – you know, the way old people do.'

Muriel Fazackerley of Hertfordshire Age Concern agreed: 'Swimming baths have long had lanes set aside for faster swimmers, for learners, even for people doing backstroke. But this is the first time that there'll be one for pensioners who just want to come and have a natter about their grandchildren. We expect a significant reduction in tutting incidents from younger people swerving to avoid them.'

Miss Morrison said she expected other swimming pools to follow suit. Eastbourne Council, however, have already ruled out the idea, saying that this is the only thing their pool is used for anyway, so frankly there would be no point. 'We do have different lanes for our elderly chatterers though,' said the manager, 'with clear signs indicating "Weeing" and "Non-weeing".'

GILBERT CHUCKS GEORGE; CUSTODY BATTLE OVER CONCEPT

The controversial concept artists Gilbert and George are separating after forty years together.

22 March

The big split follows months of tabloid rumour and innuendo after Britain's best-loved gay avant-garde living sculptors were spotted in bizarre artworks on their own. The official reason for the abstract divorce was given as 'artistic differences', though it has been well known in the art world that Gilbert has been increasingly influenced by the artistic style of Rolf Harris. However, it seems he was unable to persuade George that the duo's art should develop towards instant paintbrush cartoons slapped on to a big white canvas while a wobble-board played in the background.

Now a long legal battle is expected to follow over the 'living sculpture' concept, with the most likely outcome being George having custody during the week with the judge granting Gilbert access at the weekend and every other Wednesday. With neither side being prepared to back down, all the pictures in which they both appear are currently being divided down the middle.

Meanwhile, the major retrospective currently on show at Tate Modern has been rehung to reflect their new direction. 'Gilbert and Rolf' opens on Wednesday.

Dyslexic child 'was stupid as well'

23 March

The parents of a middle-class child diagnosed as 'dyslexic' have been contacted by educational psychologists who have discovered that the underperforming pupil was actually just stupid as well.

Seven-year-old Henry Bradley from Gloucester had been doing less well than many of his classmates for some time. 'We couldn't understand it,' said his mother. 'Henry comes from a supportive home where he is encouraged with his homework and has a private tutor for his maths. Eventually we had him privately assessed, and it was a great relief to us when the experts told us that Henry was dyslexic. Suddenly it all made sense.'

However, suspecting there may be more complex reasons for Henry's underachievement, the educational psychologist booked the child in for further tests and eventually made her unprecedented discovery. 'He's just dim,' said Dr Janice Trenter. 'Someone has to be.' Dr Trenter believes that there may be other dim middle-class children out there, but says that till now the education establishment has simply refused to accommodate the idea. 'There are countless toys for "Brainy Baby" or "Baby Genius", but not a single educational story tape or play centre aimed at thick kids. Why can't we have toys called "Stupid Baby" or "Dim Toddler"? It's discrimination, pure and simple.'

However, not wishing to upset Henry's parents Dr Trenter felt unable to tell them straight out that Henry was below average intelligence. Instead she persuaded the British Medical Association to recognize a new condition which she has coined 'stupidia'. The local authority have now received a letter from the family's doctor informing them of Henry's condition and henceforth when grades are assessed the school will have to take account of Henry's 'stupidia'.

'We're delighted with this new diagnosis,' said Mrs Bradley. 'It confirms what I have always suspected. Henry's actually very bright. He just suffers from "stupidia". It's inherited from the parents, apparently.'

ENGLISH PROPOSE 'SHOUTING' AS SINGLE EUROPEAN LANGUAGE

British delegates in Brussels have proposed a pan-European language be adopted across the EC along the lines of the simplified and very loud version of English that is already being widely shouted at Europeans by British tourists visiting the continent.

Proposals that French, German or Esperanto might be developed as a single Euro-language have constantly been vetoed by the British delegates,

who have now gone on to the offensive by proposing 'Shouting' as the Community's universal language. They claim it is much easier to understand, with a simple vocabulary and few grammatical rules except that the letter 'o' can be added on to any English noun to make a universal European word.

For example, 'Excuse me, please could you tell me the price of that item?' in Shouting would be: 'HOW MUCHO? Oi, mate, HOW MUCH

COSTO?' while 'Please may I have a beer?' becomes: 'Oi, Manuel! UNO BEERO!' If at first the fledgling linguist cannot grasp the basics of Shouting, the fluent speaker will simply reiterate, but to facilitate understanding, will say it much, much louder: 'I SAID, UNO BEERO! ARE YOU FOOKIN' DEAF OR WOT?'

Extolling the versatility of the dialect, British MEP Kenneth Smithson (UKIP) explained, 'Shouting is a genuinely international language in that it also employs words from all the major Indo-European dialects, which are pretty well interchangeable at will.' Or, as he said when he used the language to propose the motion in the European Parliament: 'WE BRITISHERS, JA? SPEAKA DA LINGO EURO, ENGLISHER FOR TOUTO EVERYONE, SÍ?' Undaunted by the puzzled looks of the various nationalities, Smithson gave an exasperated sigh and started again: 'It's quite simple, chaps. LINGO, SÍ? PARLEZ MUCHO LOUDER, JA? SHOUTY-SHOUTY, COMPRENEZ?'

Eventually a Dutch minister interjected: 'My sincere apologies for the discourteous interruption, but we're rather struggling to comprehend your vernacular. I don't suppose you speak English by any chance, do you?'

Isle of Wight iPod factory 'never stood a chance'

26 March

Attempts to turn the Isle of Wight into an economic power-house and global manufacturing centre to rival the Republic of China have foundered with the closure of Shanklin's only iPod factory.

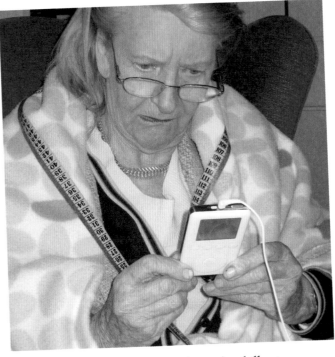

Deidre Ainsworth, head of the Isle of Wight Development Agency, still believes that the island can become what she calls the 'Wight Tiger' to rival the Pacific Rim economies or India and China, but she has been criticized for giving grants to overwhelmed pensioner groups, assuring them that they could help make the Isle of Wight the digital powerhouse of the West.

'Sure, the closure of the island's only iPod factory is a blow. People are saying I shouldn't have set up an advanced micro-technology plant in an old people's home. Well, of course it's very easy to say that now.'

In global terms the electronic assembly plant was a small concern, with one iPod being put together every couple of weeks in a former post office. The Isle of Wight's business start-up grants have more traditionally been for bed and breakfasts, tea rooms and gift shops, but Deidre Ainsworth believed the island needed to move with the times: 'Japan is an island and look what they achieved making radios and suchlike after the war.'

Nevertheless, the experiment suggests that the Isle of Wight's population may not have the skill sets required for cutting-edge technology development. 'All our residents are retired folk who struggle with this advanced digital business,' said day-care nurse Jennifer Carter at the Shanklin Sea View retirement home where the doomed iPod factory was located. 'They can't read the tiny instruction booklets even with their glasses. They want to play carpet bowls, drink tea and have an afternoon nap, they don't want to be assembling iPods at their age.'

Deidre Ainsworth, however, is undeterred. 'I believe the Isle of Wight could be the new Vegas.' Pole-dancing auditions start on Monday.

SCOOBY-DOO KIDS 'BEAT SUSPECTS INTO CONFESSION'

28 March

The crime-fighting kids made famous by the *Scooby-Doo* TV series secured false confessions through violence and intimidation, according to new papers released this week.

The claim has been made by lawyers working for the acquittal of the so-called 'Scooby-Doo 86', the large number of ageing prisoners in jail since the 1970s who all claim they were framed by the 'meddling kids and their dog'. They point to strikingly similar patterns in each account of their convoluted crimes, and the fact that the only stranger the kids ever met was always the person whom they fingered at the end.

'On screen the kids from Mystery Inc. appeared to be likeable and humorous teenagers with a strong sense of right and wrong, prepared to enter scary situations to do their bit to fight crime,' said Mike McLone, a human-rights lawyer working for the campaigning prisoners. 'In reality, Freddie and Shaggy regularly beat innocent suspects into a pulp behind the scenes, then got them to make on-screen confessions having dressed them up in a ghost costume with a removable head.'

'All the ghostly paraphernalia supposedly employed by the master criminals to scare people away from their lair – it was all set up by these desperate, attention-seeking kids,' he added. The tactics, if true, certainly worked, with Fred, Daphne, Velma, Shaggy and Scooby becoming household names for their astonishingly successful run at exposing elaborate and bizarre crimes. 'Think about it. Not once did it turn out that nothing suspicious was happening. Hundreds of innocent old men looking after slightly spooky buildings were convicted of invented crimes, just so these kids could reap all the glory.'

The kids from Mystery Inc. stepped down from crime-fighting some years ago, although no official explanation was ever given for their sudden retirement. In an official statement, their lawyers said: 'These accusations are, um, being invented by Old Man Johnson, who is, er, using the legend of the headless horseman to scare folks away from the disused goldmine. Yeah.' However, they refused to comment on allegations that Fred always sent Shaggy and Velma in the opposite direction because he was knocking off Daphne in the Mystery Machine.

Scooby was put to sleep when he became incontinent in 1991. Shaggy was busted for drug possession in 1998, while Velma now lives with her lesbian partner in Canada.

TODDLERS ADMIT FAILED STRATEGY IN WAR ON PIGEONS

29 March

Three-year-old Timmy Frampton admitted that toddlers were not winning the War on Pigeons and a new strategy was required if the conflict was to be resolved.

'For too long our tactics have been to run at the pigeons with our arms outstretched, screaming. This has proved a miscalculation,' he said, addressing cross-legged representatives of local playgroups. 'The pigeons have a superior air force, to be sure, but we have far greater strength during a ground offensive. The pigeons often run for a few feet before taking off just before we can get hold of them. If we can stop them from flying away we will have them.'

Frampton emphasized the need for more children to patrol the streets in search of anything they suspect to be a pigeon and run at it at a slightly slower pace, trying really hard not to laugh. He also assured the other pre-schoolers that Operation Stamping on the Ground to Make a Flock of Pigeons Fly up at the Same Time was proving successful and would continue on the walk home from school, prompting applause and some juice-spillage.

Despite the generally positive reaction to the proposed new strategy, dissent was heard from some quarters. One child was heard questioning what they would do if they ever actually caught a pigeon, while another was heckled for suggested the War on Pigeons was taking time and resources from other more pressing concerns such as sand-eating and mixing up the plasticine colours. With the discontent threatening to get out of hand, Frampton was forced to close the conference early, saying everyone was getting 'over-tired'.

COMPUTER NEWS ROUND-UP

YOUNG PEOPLE UNIMPRESSED BY WEBSITE SPELLING 'KIDS' WITH A 'Z'

Attempts to fool young people into thinking an educational website was cool and vaguely subversive by using the letter 'z' on the end of plurals has totally failed, it has emerged.

'Gr8-stuff-4-da-kidz.com' is in fact a government initiative to make its National Curriculum available online in a form that it was hoped would be appealing to teenagers. But the thinly disguised *educational* website has attracted only three visitors and all of these are thought to be parents trying to help their children with their homework.

'We simply can't understand it,' said a government education spokesman. 'We hired specially trained linguists to spell everything wrong and use numbers when words would be far easier to understand. We told them the site was jam-packed "wiv loadza gr8 bitz 4 da kool kidz" but the students seemed to take one look at it and decide it was not cool at all. Even using colons and brackets to make those sideways smiley faces failed to persuade them.'

In fact the only significant traffic on the site has been on the message board from teenagers complaining about the basic mistakes in spelling and grammar. 'Your phrase "Tlk2ul8r" contains no less than eight basic spelling and punctuation mistakes,' said Jordan, an excluded pupil from Hackney currently serving his third ASBO. 'Frankly, I'm appalled.'

PAPERCLIP FROM WORD QUITS MICROSOFT FOR APPLE

The IT world was plunged into controversy last night after it emerged that the animated paperclip from Microsoft Word has been headhunted by Apple and has now 'jumped ship' to work for the company. This high-profile betrayal by one of Microsoft's most trusted lieutenants is seen as a major embarrassment for the company.

'It's a logical move for us to make,' stated Steve Jobs, Apple's CEO. 'Clippy is a professional, and his knowledge of laying out letters and punctuation tips is second to none. You may think he's just an annoying bit of office stationery, but don't be fooled – this is one high-powered individual with a remarkable vision for business.'

Clippy's former colleagues, Rocky the dog and the small scientist character, refused to comment on allegations that Clippy left after persistent workplace bullying. But Steve Ballmer, CEO for Microsoft, declared himself to be 'shocked and saddened' by the news. 'Clippy's move is a blow, but his standing with Microsoft was at a low point. He kept turning up to work late, he was often drunk, and he would slump in his chair during board meetings and make lewd comments to the receptionist. Plus he would set the alarm off every time he came through the metal detectors in the lobby. He was an irritating little bastard, to be honest.'

BLOGGER WORRIED HE IS JUST TALKING TO HIMSELF

A young man has abandoned his web-log after coming to the conclusion that no one was interested in the everyday details of his life.

'I was really excited when I started my blog,' says computer-repair specialist Aaron Bagshot. 'It felt really amazing to think that I was sharing my life and thoughts with millions of people. That all around the world people were reading the everyday details of my life. Except that they weren't.'

SWISS ARMY DEMAND BETTER WEAPONS

2 April

Soldiers in the Swiss Army are demanding more effective weaponry after centuries of being armed only with handy little penknives.

Switzerland has been forced to remain neutral in successive European conflicts, including the Second World War, when it was feared that a small national force armed only with pocket knives featuring corkscrews and toothpicks might prove ineffective against Hitler's massed Panzer divisions.

But now the soldiers in Switzerland's armed forces are protesting at the humiliation of training and parading armed only with little red penknives. 'Training is rubbish,' said Karl-Heinz Schmidt of the 4th Mountain Tweezers Division. 'Last week we had to crawl on our bellies towards a stable, then storm inside and get a stone out of a horse's hoof. Later, we were shown how to use our weapons to keep our toenails short and open a bottle of lemonade.'

The Swiss Defence Minister defended their army's traditional weaponry, pointing out that their élite special forces also have a little cuticle-pusher and letter-opener. After much debate, however, the country is resolved to embark upon a major modernization of its armaments programme, which will make Switzerland one of the world's major military powers. Airports have been warned to be extra vigilant towards travellers carrying penknives with pull-out tactical nuclear weapons.

7 April

Vatican officials have called an urgent council to try and settle the Catholic's official stance on gay divorce. Since new legislation allowed gay couples to enter civil partnerships, thousands of same-sex couples have become 'married' despite fierce opposition from the Catholic Church. However, with the first legal separations of gay couples now taking place, the Vatican has been unable to decide whether to stand by its historic opposition to divorce or whether they should welcome and indeed encourage the failure of same-sex marriage.

'It's a really difficult one for us,' said Cardinal Foyle from Galway. 'We are opposed to these homosexuals being allowed to marry. But we also maintain that marriage is for life. Are we pleased that the sin of gay marriage is atoned for, or do we pray for those who are considering the sin of divorce? I'm fucked if I know.'

There are factions in the Vatican that would like to have all gay people executed and any children, adopted or otherwise, taken into care. Others are more tolerant, urging the Church to engage with the gay community. During a recent synod, the argument became so heated that several bishops got involved in an ugly fist-fight and had to be separated with their crooks.

'Do two wrongs make a right? Why does the Bible say that a man shall love his fellow man, but then not allow that other stuff? What if a man has a gay partner who then has a sex-change so the love is between a man and his ladyboy wife? Is there a website where I can learn more about this?'

British labour market flooded by workers from Narnia

9 April

GOVERNMENT FIGURES RELEASED TODAY REVEAL THAT TENS OF THOUSANDS OF ECONOMIC MIGRANTS ARE FLOODING INTO BRITAIN FROM NARNIA.

Beavers, fauns and over-allegorical lions are working long hours for low wages on building sites, in the service industries and as farm workers, causing a certain amount of resentment in some areas of the country.

Along with Romania and Bulgaria, Narnia joined the European Community on 1 January despite worries about the human-rights record of the White Witch and an ongoing diplomatic row over the whereabouts of four British children. Romanians and Bulgarians have come in smaller numbers than anticipated and have blended into the British workforce almost unnoticed. However, thousands of Narnians arriving via a wardrobe in an unspecified English country house have not found it so easy to blend in to British society, since they are talking mammals or mythical creatures such as giants and witches. A building-site manager in Ipswich said, 'We've got a few Narnians on the site. There's a satyr, a stag and I think that nattering beaver is from Narnia as well. They're good workers, but all that sixth-form symbolism gets on the other lads' tits from time to time . . .'

In Market Harborough, a group of local youths got into a fracas with a number of Narnians, calling them 'Faunies', pushing and shoving and saying that none of the books were as good as the first one. Eventually police had to be called after one of the locals was turned into a stone statue.

Now there are calls for limits to be put on the number of Narnian workers coming into the country. However, they have been defended by one New Labour MP who admits to employing a Narnian handyman. 'He's marvellous,' said Dawn McHugh. 'Not only does he do the gardening, decorating and odd jobs around the house, but he also lays down his life for the children before the epic climactic battle between good and evil. Why can't British workers do that?'

ENGLAND RUGBY FANS IN SHOCK AS MORE LINES DISCOVERED TO 'SWING LOW, SWEET CHARIOT'

11 April

England rugby fans were reeling today at the shock news that musicologists have discovered that 'Swing Low, Sweet Chariot' does in fact have more than two lines. Ian James, the lead researcher, said, 'It seems that the song is not, as was thought, an endless chant for boorish, ex-public schoolboys to bray when the England team is winning, but an African-American spiritual originating in the slave community of the Deep South. The irony of this would be almost unbearable, if the rugby fans had the modicum of intellectual sensitivity required to see it.'

Fraser 'Diggers' Digby, City trader and keen England rugby supporter said, 'Apparently the other lines have something to do with Jordan, but I thought she was calling herself Katie Price these days.'

Parents worried that toddler isn't texting yet

13 April

Anxious parents Alan and Natalie Easter from Southend are contacting health and educational professionals after becoming increasingly concerned about the lack of communication skills displayed by their two-year-old daughter.

'She's had a mobile phone since she was six months old, but she still hasn't written her first text message,' they explained. To give her a head start with her communication

skills, the couple have avoided talking directly to her, bombarding her with SMS messages instead in the hope that she will pick up the language that way. 'We've sent her picture texts and smiley emoticons but we just feel we are not getting anything back.'

The girl, called K8, is now undergoing a series of psychometric tests and cognitive-ability checks to ascertain whether her communication issues are part of a wider problem with her intellectual development. 'K8's older brother and sister were way ahead of K8 by this age,' recalls her mother.

Kvn, the eldest of the Easter children, wrote his first words aged just eighteen months. Natalie recalls how she awoke at 3 a.m. to find the message 'I ve 2 p' from their first child. His mother then frantically texted 'omg' to her husband and the couple exchanged a further series of joyful electronic communications on the subject, and only five minutes later a second message arrived, saying 'sry 2 l8'.

'I'd not actually seen him "ftf" since I'd recharged his phone the week before and rushed to his room at which he asked me "hu d f r u?" It was magical. And I'm just not getting anything like that from my daughter. The doctors have tried asking her what's wrong, and why she is being so uncooperative. But she wouldn't reply to their MSN messages either.'

Old lady who swallowed a horse 'should have been stopped earlier'

15 April

The death of a care-in-the-community patient who collapsed this week after attempting to swallow a horse has been described by mental-health experts as a tragedy that should have been averted.

The old lady, Mrs Teasdale from Lewisham in south-east London, was judged 'not to be a danger to herself or others', even after she had swallowed a series of sizeable farm animals. Defending Lewisham Social Services, Councillor Bryan Clarkson said, 'When this case first came to our attention, all we knew was that there was an old lady who swallowed a fly. I don't know why she swallowed a fly. It was suggested that perhaps she'll die, though at that stage it seemed unlikely.'

Subsequent warnings, however, that the old lady had swallowed a spider to catch the fly, and then swallowed a bird to catch the spider, should have set off alarm bells, according to the department's critics. Yet their only reaction to the news that the old lady had swallowed a cat to catch the bird was 'Fancy

Banksy didn't draw *Naked Lady with Big Bosoms*

17 April

A piece of street art thought to have been created by the famous Banksy was not in fact the work of the cult street artist, according to experts from Sotheby's.

Naked Lady with Big Bosoms was originally thought to be the latest urban artwork from the elusive graffiti genius and was quickly snapped up for an undisclosed seven-figure sum. 'It features the image of a naked woman with great emphasis placed upon the breasts and pubic hair,' said Marc Casper from Tate Modern. 'It is clearly a statement about the objectification of the female body; it has beauty yet sadness, it attracts yet repels. I cannot believe it is not the work of Banksy.'

However, art historians are adamant that the work is not genuine and point to witnesses who saw a twelve-year-old boy with a spray can running away from the location just before the 'new Banksy masterpiece' was discovered. New York collectors are now seeking authentication of other recent 'Banksy' purchases such as *Man with Large Nose Looking over Wall* and *Big Cock with Hairy Balls.*

that, she swallowed a cat!' when in fact she should have been sectioned under the Mental Health Act 1983. Further bizarre feats of compulsive swallowing were blithely accepted as normal behaviour: Mrs Teasdale swallowed a goat, which wouldn't catch a dog in any case; and then a cow – obviously a herbivore and useless at catching a goat at the best of times. By the time she swallowed a horse it was simply too late and the coroner declared the old lady dead: 'of course.'

'This litany of neglect is a damning indictment of Lewisham's Social Services Department,' he added. 'At each stage, Mrs Teasdale should have been given appropriate mental and medical attention; instead she was just left to continue swallowing these animals under the tragic misapprehension that each would somehow catch the last one – when it is clear that her plan was seriously flawed on several fronts.'

The real tragedy, according to medical experts, is that the original fly would have been killed by Mrs Teasdale's stomach acid, thereby rendering any further swallowing completely pointless.

BANK TO INTRODUCE 'NEAR ENOUGH' PIN TECHNOLOGY

19 April

Barclays Bank has today announced measures to ensure that customers can withdraw cash from machines as long as they get fairly close with their PIN number.

A spokesman for the high street bank said, 'A lot of people have trouble remembering their wife's birthday, never mind their PIN number. In future, as long as people get two or three digits correct in approximately the right order we will allow the transaction.'

There will, however, be a sliding scale of payments. If you get only two digits out of four, you only get half the money requested. If you get three correct you get most of the money and a chance to order a new cheque book. Extra allowance is to be made for mistakes after closing time on Friday and Saturday nights, said Barclays. Failure to get any numbers correct will be met with a helpful response along the lines of: 'Come on, it must be the same number you use for everything – try the year you were born, you pissed bastard.'

SOHO SAUNA PARLOURS OFFERING 'EGO MASSAGE'

20 April

A discreet new service is being offered in unlicensed sauna parlours in London as men pay attractive young women good money to give them an 'ego massage'.

'Our typical customer is a lonely, low-achieving man, probably on a dull business trip to the capital,' said one ego masseur. 'He's probably just failed to secure some crucial contract so he comes in here, lies down on the slab and then one of the girls will ask him if he works out a lot, what's he going to do when he hits thirty and then she'll laugh long and hard at his golfing anecdotes.'

'It's kind of a tension release,' explained Mr X, who wished to remain anonymous since his real name is Kevin. 'If I'm feeling a bit low, like no one thinks I'm any good, then I go in there and the girls are really impressed when I tell them about my new Sat Nav. One of them actually asked if I would bring it with me next time I came in.'

But ego massages remain illegal in the UK and one covert police recording recently revealed some of the other methods used. The short and balding customer was clearly wearing an ill-fitting BHS suit which the ego masseur suggested must be an Armani. Then, on discovering that her customer was a regional distributor for photocopying supplies in the South-West region, she affected astonishment as she had just been talking to someone who said how excellently photocopying supplies were distributed in the Plymouth area.

At this point the police burst in, shouting, 'Nobody move!' The ego masseur commended the officer for his naturally authoritative manner, asked him if he had ever thought of doing any professional voice work, and the conversation continued for another half an hour or so. No charges were ultimately brought.

Corner-takers' secret arm signals 'finally decoded'

22 April

The secret semaphore-like messages given by footballers taking corner kicks have finally been deciphered by a team of top code-breakers from MI5.

For years soccer fans have been intrigued by the significance of the single raised arm gesture from a player just before he takes the corner kick. Sometimes he would raise his left arm, sometimes his right; then the code grew yet more complex when players began occasionally raising both arms. Yet despite years of analysis, the secret meaning of these puzzling hand signals remained unknown to all except the players' team-mates. Until now, when the greatest mathematical and psychological minds have finally emerged from years spent studying recordings of Premiership football matches, and cross-checking the messages with the subsequent strategy of the players.

'We have cracked it!' announced the excited MI5 agent known only as 'K'. 'The code was based on a complex cryptographic algorithm, but now we can share it with the outside world. If a player raises his right arm it means: "I am going to kick the ball into the penalty area." If he raises his left arm it means: "I am going to kick the ball into the penalty area." And if he raises both arms it means: "I am going to kick the ball into the penalty area. Try and score a goal."'

There was dismay among Premiership players that the secrets had been made public and now an entirely new secret code will have to be devised. During training for their forthcoming Premiership clash with Chelsea, Manchester United players were seen practising for corners, making the shape of a tea pot before the kick, as well as banging their fists on their foreheads and doing the dance from 'The Birdie Song'. Then they kicked the ball into the penalty area.

Mr Men publisher launches 'Mr Hoody'

MR. HOODY

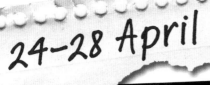

Italian waiter with normal-sized pepper mill disappoints hen party

24 April

A hen party was shocked into silence this week as the Italian waiter serving their pizzas produced a standard three-inch pepper mill, leaving the group of girls unable to hide their disappointment.

No amount of novelty devils' horns and chocolate willies could raise a smile afterwards.

Chloe from Braintree in Essex, who is to be a bridesmaid at her sister Sharon's wedding, was scathing: 'Well, we were stunned, to be honest. It's supposed to be part of the fun. One of us will normally shout, "Oh, what a big one," and the rest of the girls fall about laughing. It never fails . . . It's a reference to his knob, you see.'

Instead the disappointed hen party endured an awkward silence, while the waiter looked embarrassed and ashamed. 'We felt a bit sorry for him. It kind of took away the buzz we had created by flashing our bras out the roof of the white stretch limo on the way there.'

Experienced waiter Mario Perrone, who has been working at the Little Italy pizzeria for two years, was insistent that he does in fact possess an enormous pepper mill but that 'one of the other waiters must have hidden it as some kind of joke. I felt humiliated,' he added. 'I felt like a failure as a man.'

A few attempts at innuendo were made when it was noticed that the menu mentioned 'dough balls' and 'Italian sausage' but the atmosphere around the table never really recovered. However, the barman at Dreamz nightclub later saved the night with a cheeky response to Sharon's request for a 'Sloe Comfortable Screw against the Wall'. The girls' laughter continued for some time.

'Degsy' from Redditch tops UK Skint List

26 April

An unemployed 27-year-old from Redditch tops the prestigious *Sunday Sport* Skint List, which was published yesterday.

Although registered at his parents' house 'for tax reasons', Derek 'Degsy' O'Rourke has a number of homes across the West Midlands area, most notably his brother's spare room and his ex-girlfriend's car, for which he still possesses a key, and in which he often sleeps if he passes it on the way home from the pub.

Last year Mr O'Rourke was only fourth in the UK Skint List, but since then a number of his investments have failed to materialize, most notably a scratch-card, which he had promised his creditors was 'definitely the big one', and a number of empty cider bottles which his dad told him would fetch a penny each if he took them down the off licence. Degsy's total assets, including a dried-out packet of Old Holborn and a jumper, are estimated to be worth around 37p. During the last financial year his total earnings were 40p, which he accumulated by kicking the Copper Cascade machine at the funfair before being kicked out.

A spokesman for Britain's skintest man said: 'Mr O'Rourke prefers not to comment on his financial situation, in case you are the people from the social.'

'He might speak to you when he wakes up if you give him a quid,' added his local priest, 'but he's been asleep on my sofa for two days after finding where I had hidden all the communion wine.'

Second on this year's *Sunday Sport* Skint List was 'performance anarchist' Dave 'Dogbreath' Thomas from Bristol, who said, 'Money is just their way of trying to enslave you; I won't have nothing to do with them bread-heads' mind control. Can you lend me a tenner?' Third was the founder of holiday company Baghdad Breaks PLC and in joint fourth place were former pop duo Bros.

GOVERNMENT ADMIT TO LOSING THE ISLE OF WIGHT

28 April

The government came under fierce criticism today for losing the Isle of Wight, which is believed to have disappeared some time last month, although its absence has apparently only just been noticed.

The mislaying of the diamond-shaped island was actually uncovered by the leader of the opposition, who had intended to visit during his campaign for the local elections. David Cameron set off by boat yesterday morning from Southampton, but after heading out into the Solent and rowing around for some time he realized that the island was no longer there. 'This is typical of the incompetence that we have come to expect from this government,' he said in the House of Commons later that day. 'Not only have they lost a beautiful and much-loved part of England, but it seems that they weren't even aware that they had lost it! Shouldn't the minister responsible either find the island or have the decency to resign?'

A Downing Street spokesman said that enormous efforts are already under way to locate the popular tourist destination, including a large number of photocopied notices that have been tied on to lampposts in the Southampton area. However, the House of Commons did not seem over-concerned and MPs soon moved on to other business.

43

HUBBLE TELESCOPE DISCOVERS NEW SIGN OF THE ZODIAC

1 May

In the most exciting development in astrology for hundreds of years, new pictures have revealed a new sign of the zodiac: the Duck-Billed Platypus.

On joining up the three stars, astrologers were amazed at the uncanny resemblance to the elusive egg-laying mammal, and so the Duck-Billed Platypus becomes the first new sign of the zodiac since Galileo discovered Capricorn in 1611. Astrologists say the discovery has finally solved an ancient mystery about certain 'platypus-like' attributes of those born on the cusp of Aries and Taurus. 'You lucky Platypuses are stubborn, sociable and good with your hands. You enjoy the company of others but sometimes need to be on your own,' said former TV astrologer Russell Grant.

A spokesman from NASA added: 'These photos confirm the existence of three stars that have been known about for some time. I never imagined these kooks would start making all these crazy claims. But that's me all over, I suppose – typical Platypus.'

Queen swears oath of allegiance to teenage gang

3 May

The government's citizenship plans were in disarray this week when it emerged that plans for school-leavers to swear an oath of allegiance to Her Majesty had been outflanked by the Queen herself swearing an oath to a south London street gang.

The Brixton posse known as the Crips, based on the Los Angeles gang of the same name, gained their newest member at a private ceremony behind some lock-up garages near Clapham North tube station. Baring her forearm to allow a local gangleader to fashion an amateur tattoo, Her Majesty pledged to uphold the honour of the Crips Set and 'kill da bad-ass Blood Set mothers'.

Certain royal engagements, such as a meeting of the Commonwealth Enterprise Forum, had to be postponed while Her Majesty undertook new responsibilities, including tagging a railway bridge and standing on street corners selling small amounts of crack-cocaine.

k. d. lang changes name to K. D. Lang

5 May

Pop star k. d. lang has announced she is changing her name to K. D. Lang in a bid to woo more mature fans. 'The lower-case letters have been great for K. D.,' said her manager, 'but she has grown as an artist and feels that perhaps there's an older type of fan out there who might be more comfortable with correct punctuation. Plus it was a real pain always correcting the bank or whatever.'

But the controversial name-change has caused anger among long-standing fans. 'Who the hell is this "K. D. Lang", for God's sake?' wept one devotee from the singer's home town of Consort, Alberta. 'Lower case says rebellion, anti-establishment and texting. These capital letters represent a massive betrayal. I don't care what she starts calling herself, she'll always be k. d. lang to us.'

One emotional caller to a rock-music phone-in described it as one of the greatest sell-outs in the history of rock and roll: '1958: Elvis goes into the army; 1965: Dylan goes electric; 2006: k. d. lang goes upper-case.'

LLOYD WEBBER SEEKING CONTESTANTS FOR REALITY CRUCIFIXION SHOW

8 May

The BBC today revealed plans for a new reality show in which Andrew Lloyd Webber will seek out someone 'special' from among the general public to take on the coveted but currently vacant role of absolver of all our sins.

The show, entitled *They Know Not What They Do*, has received thousands of applications but only two exceptionally true and loving contestants will make it to the final where the prize of a long, slow, tragic but profoundly symbolic death by crucifixion on prime-time TV awaits.

The successful contestant, who Lloyd Webber conceded would probably drive a Toyota Prius, would shame us all by dying on the cross because of our indifference to the plight of those less fortunate, and our extensive use of plastic bags. 'Through his noble self-sacrifice we'll be able to carry on exactly as before,' he said. 'But he'd be there in our minds at all times, urging us to do the right thing and reminding everyone what great telly it was that night.'

Producers have rejected an offer of having common criminals executed on either side of the winner. 'Nice though it was of the Home Office to get into the spirit of the show . . .'

45

Cameron apes Radiohead with 'pay as much tax as you want'

9 May

The Conservative Party has committed itself to a radical new tax policy in which wage earners only have to hand over as much money to the exchequer as they think is appropriate.

Inspired by last year's innovative release of Radiohead's new album 'In Rainbows' for which music fans could choose their own price, the Tory front bench believe they have really hit upon a vote-winning economic policy.

'We've done the sums and they definitely add up,' said Conservative leader David Cameron. 'We reckon that people will probably choose to voluntarily surrender around thirty per cent of their income, which should be enough to run all the schools and hospitals and stuff.'

'Obviously some people might opt to pay no tax at all,' conceded George Osborne, 'but we're confident that lots of other people will decide to pay much, much more than they are paying at the moment. What's so thrilling is that it really involves ordinary people in decisions about setting their own tax thresholds!' added the excited shadow chancellor.

On the streets of Britain's marginal constituencies, voters responded positively to so-called 'Radiohead Economics'; 'Let's see now: I've got two kids at state schools, I use the local hospital, then there's all the other stuff like my parents' pension, the lads in Iraq, the arts and everything . . . ' said one taxpayer. 'So I reckon I would probably hand over about, er, nothing. Yeah that sounds about right.'

NHS life support to be decided on penalties

11 May

National Health patients in comas or dependent on expensive long-term care will no longer be kept on life-support machines indefinitely. The matter of life or death will now be decided on penalties, it was announced yesterday.

'With an increasingly ageing population, we simply cannot go on keeping more and more terminally ill people in intensive care,' said Health Minister Alan Johnson. 'We have been trying to settle on a fair way of choosing which machines to switch off, and decided that penalties was a system that people understood and considered to be just.'

Under the scheme, the spouse of the patient on life support will have to face five penalties taken by junior doctors. He or she will then have to take five penalties against the hospital accountant, and if the scores are still even, then it will go to 'sudden death'.

Unfortunately, in a recent pilot scheme, Mrs Agnes Johnson, the elderly wife concerned, argued with the referee and was sent off, leaving her unconscious husband to face the penalties in her place while lying on a hospital trolley.

Commentating on the life-or-death shoot-out, John Motson said, 'You can understand why the tension might be getting to the goalie – there's an awful lot at stake here this afternoon. But that's no excuse for ill discipline on the field of play.'

One opposition health spokesman has criticized the scheme: 'It is ridiculous that something as important as a patient's life is decided by simply taking penalties. The player should at the very least have to dribble from the halfway line and beat a defender or something . . . '

Umbrellas escaping from owners 'deliberately'

13 May

New footage from CCTV cameras has revealed that thousands of small portable umbrellas are intentionally escaping from their owners and slipping away to join other stray brollies living in the wild.

Most people blame themselves when they lose an umbrella for not having remembered it when they left the café or bus. But it turns out that the reason why they didn't notice it is that the umbrella had already crept under their chair and away to freedom. Now thousands of so-called 'urban umbrellas' are adapting to a new life in our inner cities, congregating in large packs in abandoned wasteland, where lucky enthusiasts claim to have seen them stretching out and soaking up the sun's rays.

'They actually hate the rain,' explains keen umbrella-watcher Ken Millington. 'That's the main reason why they escape from captivity – because people never take them out in the sunshine. But to spot a wild umbrella in a park or a back garden stretching out just as the sun comes up is an amazing sight.'

Occasionally the umbrellas will slip into litter bins or gutters, where they will lie completely still if a passer-by comes near. However, some local councils are concerned that the wild-umbrella population is getting out of control and is posing a threat to other urban inhabitants. 'Unless we take steps to cull our stray umbrella population now, wild shopping trolleys and individual gloves on railings may soon be driven to extinction.'

BIRDWATCHERS THRILLED AT FIRST-EVER SIGHTING OF A GIRLFRIEND

<u>15 May</u>

Hundreds of excited twitchers converged on a remote Welsh estuary yesterday where a fellow birdwatcher was spotted with a girlfriend.

Ornithologists think this may be the first-ever sighting of a birdwatcher's girlfriend on the British mainland.

'Isn't she a beauty!' said Ray Meader, 57. 'I've seen drawings and photos before but I've never seen one for real.' The girlfriend was clearly visible on the far shoreline, holding the hand of a young male birdwatcher, having a drink and, to the gasps of watching twitchers, giving him a kiss.

But hopes that the pair might breed in Britain were sadly dashed. After a couple of hours of being photographed and stared at by middle-aged men in anoraks the girlfriend suddenly fled, leaving the young male birdwatcher looking confused and disorientated for a few minutes.

Later he spotted a guillemot and perked up again.

Global 'credit crunch' blamed for neighbour's refusal to lend lawnmower

<u>16 May</u>

A Norfolk man has blamed the global credit crunch and sub-prime debacle as justification for refusing to lend his lawnmower to his 84-year-old neighbour.

Council worker Derek Sharp, 48, said he 'wasn't prepared to compromise his assets' during what he described as 'this period of uncertainty and turbulence'.

NEO-NAZI SKINHEADS FEEL 'EVERYONE IS AGAINST THEM'

<u>17 May</u>

A SPOKESMAN FOR A GROUP OF NEO-NAZI SKINHEADS FROM FORMER EAST GERMANY SAYS MANY OF HIS FRIENDS ARE SUFFERING FROM DEPRESSION BROUGHT ON BY BEING TREATED AS SOCIAL OUTCASTS.

'People see the shaven head, the jackboots and the swastika tattoo on the forehead and they make all sorts of assumptions,' said Adolf Blitzkreig (not his real name). 'I applied for a job at Disneyland and I didn't even get a second interview. Everyone is against us, but we're just regular guys who just happen to love our fatherland and a certain style of retro clothing,' he told assembled journalists at a Dresden press conference organized on the anniversary of Hitler's birthday.

'Why is it acceptable to be prejudiced against neo-Nazis, but not Jews, who incidentally have masterminded an international conspiracy to take over the world and organized 9/11?' At this point there were groans from the assembled journalists who began to walk out or shout: 'Racist shithead!'

'You see?' blurted an emotional Adolf. 'You're just the same as the rest of them.'

PAEDOPHILE FURIOUS AS COMPUTER IS RETURNED WITH ICONS REARRANGED

<u>18 May</u>

Convicted paedophile Edward Hulfer was threatening to launch a legal action against the Metropolitan Police this week after his computer was returned to him with his desktop tidied up and the icons arranged neatly in columns on the left-hand side of the screen.

'It's an outrageous infringement of my personal liberties,' said the convicted sex offender, who has been regularly questioned by police since his original conviction in the 1980s. 'It wasn't just the icons, they had reset the clock, changed the colour scheme and resized the screen. I feel like it doesn't belong to me any more.'

Mr Hulfer has appealed to *The Sun* to launch a campaign on behalf of sex offenders who have had their computers changed in this way, but was disappointed when his 'Save Our Paedos' Laptops' campaign was not taken up by Britain's biggest-selling tabloid. However, the unfair treatment has left him feeling that society might start to see him as a victim rather than a threat. 'OK, so what I did was wrong. But what the police have done to my computer is wrong too. I feel it sort of evens things out.'

49

PORN MAG PUBLISHER LAUNCHES LEADERS' WIVES

LEADERS' WIVES — Edition One

HOT FIRST LADY ACTION!!

FEATURE: Shhh! Don't tell my husband, but I'm 'voting for the other side'

The Babes of Eastern Europe

19 May

Soft-core publishers Galaxy are launching a new specialty magazine featuring explicit private photos sent in by prime ministers and presidents from around the world.

Leaders' Wives magazine will not reveal the identity of the various first ladies from around the globe, although according to the magazine's editor 'part of the fun will be guessing'.

Edition One features 'A Lovely English Lass' and 'A Gorgeous Gallic Gal' pictured together exchanging what is euphemistically entitled 'an intimate exchange on the challenges of being in the public eye'.

The idea has been under consideration for some time, said editor Jonny Barfield: 'We did publish a pilot edition of *Leaders' Wives* back in the early 1990s but had to pulp thousands of copies containing explicit pics of Norma Major and Barbara Bush.' But with politicians' partners becoming more and more attractive, the hope is that *Leaders' Wives* magazine will combine a growing interest in global political issues with the ever-popular topic of soft-core pornography.

There will also be fantasy letters from leading politicians, under headings such as 'Massive Election' and 'I Screwed the Voters', and if Hillary Clinton has another go at the US Presidency, the magazine also promises an explicit new feature entitled 'One for the Ladies', says Barfield. 'Although most of the women in Washington, DC, will have seen that already, at one time or another.'

20 May

The Home Office this week announced they are introducing a power-tools amnesty that allows men to hand in dangerous power tools that they have no idea how to use safely.

'These lethal tools can be handed in anonymously, with no questions asked,' said the Home Secretary. 'The owners can avoid the humiliation of other men knowing they cannot cope with power saws, high-speed drills and electric sanders, and their wives will never know the presents have been returned.'

Government announce power-tools amnesty

2012 OLYMPIC ORGANIZERS CONFIDENT OF FIASCO

21 May

Organizers of London's 2012 Olympics say that plans are well on course to deliver the humiliating opening-day debacle that is expected of them.

'We're all too aware that the eyes of the world will be upon us, but we're confident that we can provide the monumentally spectacular cock-up that the nation, indeed the world, expects from us,' said Tobias Graham, joint vice deputy head of the Chaos Management co-coordinating subcommittee.

'We only have one chance to get this wrong, and with that in mind we're already working round the clock to eliminate any possibility whatsoever of the opening ceremony passing without a hitch.' Mr Graham refused to be drawn on the exact nature of the jaw-droppingly basic errors currently being proposed, but planners are believed to be considering a number of options, such as forgetting to fit the main Olympic Stadium with doors; building the entire swimming arena upside down at a secret location in Canada; or releasing eight al-Qaeda terrorists from prison so that they can join Jade Goody in lighting the Olympic torch. There are also believed to be contingency plans to ensure that the national anthems of bitter enemies such as Israel and Iran are 'accidentally' swapped during the opening parade.

'I'm delighted to report that the construction of the velodrome is already six years behind schedule,' boasted Mr Graham, standing under the Olympic logo showing six interlocking rings, 'whilst the combined small-bore rifle and show-jumping arena has been completed ahead of time and saw its first fatality in trials only last week. Obviously, new standards of monumentally hopeless performance are being set all the time, but we are quietly confident of getting the metaphorical gold medal for incompetence. Although we're not actually doing medals this time, it'll just be certificates.'

GlaxoSmith-Kline buys Belgium

In the first merger of its kind, multinational giant GlaxoSmithKline merged with Belgium this week. The new organization will be called SmithKlineBelgium, which becomes the first global company to incorporate a nation state.

For some time, GlaxoSmithKline had been buying up large parts of Brussels, Antwerp and Bruges, but the boldness of this step still took City analysts by surprise. On the streets of Brussels this morning there were some protests at the loss of notional independence, though most Belgian citizens were delighted to learn that they will receive nine hundred euros each under the terms of the takeover.

'Belgium is exactly the right country for us,' said the President of the pharmaceutical giant. 'We get a seat at the EC Council of Ministers, membership of NATO and an endless supply of delicious chocolates. Having a small army also gives us a certain amount of leverage in the war against petty regulations and red tape.'

In a separate development Moldova took itself off the stock exchange yesterday when investors failed to meet the buying price.

'SHOW US PRETTIER GIRLS GETTING BREAST SCANS,' SAYS TOP TORY

The Conservative new health spokesman has used his first public appearance to criticize TV coverage of women being scanned for possible breast cancer.

Government to publish league tables on 'hardest' schools

26 May

The Department of Education has announced it is to publish league tables showing which schools are the best at fighting and just looking scary.

A government education minister explained: 'Parents have the right to know this information. It will help them make an informed choice on the right school for their child. Some of our lowest-achieving schools academically may have other strengths. Often the highest GCSE results come from boys who are soft as shite.'

Education unions were angry at teachers being saddled with another layer of bureaucracy as it will involve their members assessing how many hard-nuts there are in any one year group, and whether they are just all mouth or 'could actually give it some'.

Meanwhile the headmaster of Streatham Technical School claimed that some schools were distorting their data and he challenged the government figures. 'They've got us below Norwood Boys. Our lads could 'ave them no problem, they're all gay.' The headmaster has arranged a 'massive bundle' between the two schools on Streatham Common after school tomorrow to resolve the issue.

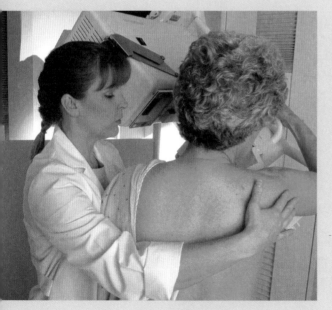

'Whenever there is a feature about breast scans, they always show some saggy old bint in her fifties with her top off,' said Peter Atherton, retired army officer and MP for Surrey West. 'There are lots of prettier young girls they could use. Why can't we see one of them with their top off instead?'

The Department of Health is keen to encourage women to get regular mammograms and has been looking at ways of raising awareness of breast-cancer issues. But the shadow minister's suggestion, made in a speech to the Royal College of Nursing, got a frosty reception, particularly when he suggested that nurses themselves could augment their wages by posing for breast-scan photos.

'This isn't about titillation or voyeurism, it's about getting the message across in the most appealing way possible,' he said afterwards. 'But if nurses kept their little hats on and sort of glanced around looking surprised, it would certainly grab my attention!'

Bottle of Tabasco sauce finished

27 May

A stunned house-wife put two drops of Tabasco into a spicy pasta sauce – and was astonished to find that the bottle was empty.

'I couldn't believe my eyes,' said Mrs Rutherford of Havant in Hampshire. 'I thought I'd made a mistake, but I'd definitely used the last of the bottle.' Mrs Rutherford's amazement was all the more intense when she realized that the bottle had been emptied a mere twelve years past its sell-by date.

SCIENTISTS IDENTIFY GENE THAT MAKES MEN LOOK ROUND AT NEW CAR

29 May

Scientists working on the Genome Project have finally identified the gene that makes men anxiously look round as they walk away from their brand-new car.

Until now, men's tendency to repeatedly glance back at their pride and joy, confirming that it was still parked where they left it five seconds earlier, was thought to be caused by some sort of social conditioning. This discovery, however, has proved the habit is caused by gene number xf4 7889g and that theoretically it would be possible to remove this gene and cure future generations of the affliction.

Sweet manufacturer introduces 'Hate Hearts'

Global warming: world leaders agree 'to cross that bridge when we come to it'

30 May

At the Reykjavik summit on climate change this week, world leaders agreed that global warming, rising sea levels and worldwide flooding are massive challenges facing mankind but are 'far enough away to be ignored for the time being'.

Amid reports that the ice caps are melting faster than previously thought, leaders of the industrialized nations expressed their grave concerns about the dangers of rising sea levels wiping out whole countries, drowning millions and completely altering the climate of planet Earth.

However, on hearing that this is all more than thirty years away, the leaders agreed to come back to the problem 'nearer the time'.

Increased cocaine use prompts Septum Donor cards

31 May

The Health Secretary this week launched a new scheme encouraging people to carry septum donor cards.

The shortage of septums for transplant has reached crisis level as more and more cocaine-users are losing the skin and gristle inside their nose. The handy new cards bear the legend 'I would like a cocaine addict to have separate nostrils after I die'.

However, it appears that the cards may come too late for celebrity cocaine-head Danniella Westbrook, who is looking to repair her nostrils again after her face rejected yet another transplant. Surgeons battled for hours to save the fragile layers of skin and gristle, but to no avail. 'They say two into one won't go,' said head surgeon Simon Andrews, 'but with Danniella's nostrils it seems to be unavoidable.'

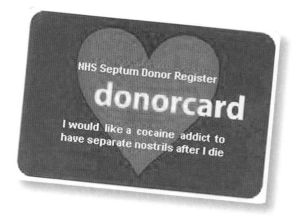

NHS Septum Donor Register
donorcard
I would like a cocaine addict to have separate nostrils after I die

Dolphins 'stop smiling the moment our backs are turned'

1 June

New evidence from unmanned underwater cameras has proved that dolphins are only pretending to be friendly to humans and that the moment that our backs are turned, a sour and indignant expression returns to their faces.

The discovery, which will traumatize animal-lovers the world over, was made when Californian marine biologist Mike Varney sensed that the smiling, chattering manner of dolphins and porpoises was somehow a little insincere. He set up a series of remote-controlled underwater cameras to record cetaceans interacting with swimmers and divers and then filmed the same dolphins as they left their human companions.

'It's fascinating,' said Varney. 'As the excited eco-tourists climb on to the boat, still thrilled at their real-life encounter with wild bottlenose dolphins, you can see the dolphins turn away and their cheerful expression suddenly changes. They look really pissed off, and are sort of tutting and looking skywards. It's like they're saying "I AM SO BORED OF THIS!"'

Varney's research has also demonstrated that their high-pitched animated chattering is also contrived and phoney. Amongst themselves, dolphins manage little more than an occasional indignant grunt, and often can't even be bothered to reply to other family members.

This is the second major discovery by maverick naturalist Varney. Last year his remote-controlled cameras discovered that gorillas are actually really smiley when they are left to themselves.

2 June

A poll published this week indicates that the new series of *Big Brother* has done an enormous amount to raise public awareness of so-called 'vacuous people'.

For years vacuous people have been shunned by the British public, who presumed that their empty-headed, cliché-riddled monologues were down to them simply being dim, uninteresting and self-obsessed individuals.

But since a number of sufferers were given the chance to compete in *Big Brother*, public awareness of their condition has greatly increased. 'It's been, like, really amazing for me, like, personally . . . ' explained Trish

Big Brother has raised public awareness of 'vacuous people'

McKinnon, who suffers from acute inanity and self-obsession. 'Like, before the series went out, like, people would hear vacuous people like me talking on the bus, yeah? And they'd just, like, take an instant dislike to me, you know? But I think I'm a beautiful person, and I'm ready to find happiness, and for me, personally, where I am in my life right now, people just have to accept the real me . . . '

At this point the interviewer shouted, 'Oh fuck off!' which Trish mistakenly put down to Tourette's Syndrome.

NEW CHESS PIECE INTRODUCED

3 June

The World Chess Federation today unveiled the new chess piece that they hope will revive flagging interest in the ancient board game. Fears that teenagers were more interested in PlayStation games such as Grand Theft Auto and Gangs of London had persuaded the WCF to update the once popular game.

After much controversy and anticipation, the new piece will be known as 'the monk'. There were gasps as the piece was unveiled before the world's media by Former Grand Master Uri Yelanov and Carol Vorderman.

'It is very exciting,' said Yelanov. 'The monk can move three spaces horizontally or diagonally and occupies the starting positions of the middle two pawns that the monks now replace. Suddenly chess is as exciting as PlayStation!'

Traditionalists, however, were highly critical of changing any of the pieces at all, as well as the plan to put sponsors' names on the chest of the king and queen. Others have criticized the monk as being too conservative. Ideas that were rejected by the World Chess Federation included 'the archer', which allowed you to cheat, 'the tardis', which could go back in time and undo stupid moves you did ten minutes ago, and 'the B52', which allowed you to blow up all your opponent's pieces before the game had even started.

Pilot flew jumbo 'without deep voice'

5 June

A BRITISH AIRWAYS 747 WAS FORCED TO MAKE AN EMERGENCY LANDING THIS MORNING WHEN THE PILOT MADE AN ANNOUNCEMENT TO PASSENGERS WITHOUT USING THE MANDATORY DEEP AND REASSURING VOICE.

Informing passengers that the weather was clear with a slight tail wind, Captain John Sitton gabbled nervously in an anxious high-pitched stutter. 'It was terrifying,' said one passenger. 'He sounded like a scared gay.'

The air crew did their best to calm passengers, urging them to return to their seats and fasten their seatbelts, but the situation deteriorated when Captain Sitton came back on the PA system and screamed at passengers that they were now flying at 'thirty thousand bloody feet!' adding: 'Fuck me, that's a long way up, isn't it? I don't understand how a massive bit of metal like this stays up in the air!'

The routine flight from Manchester to Rome was then forced to land at Paris Charles de Gaulle, where a French pilot with a really cool gravelly voice was found. British Airways have promised an inquiry. 'All our pilots are trained to sound as if they're not scared. We apologize to the customers for any inconvenience caused,' said the BA spokesman in the appropriately insincere tone of voice.

CRYSTAL METH AND PRUNES ENTER TYPICAL UK 'BASKET'

7 June

Crystal meth, crack and skunk have all been added to the typical basket of UK goods used to measure inflation, the Office for National Statistics has announced.

Speed, bennies, glue and chewing tobacco are all to be removed from goods used to measure the Retail Price Index.

Other items added to the basket include prunes, Red Bull, speed-camera fines, internet porn and TV Easy. Items removed include Spangles, Crocs shoes, library fines and Will Young CDs.

Identical twins in face-transplant success

8 June

A pair of identical twins have had each other's face successfully transplanted on to their own in the world's first ever double face transplant.

The identical twins, Don and Ron Withers from Brighton, Sussex, made medical history this week after enduring twenty-two hours of surgery under anaesthetic, but emerged looking fit and well with barely a mark to suggest the ground-breaking operation they had just been through. 'It's amazing,' said their mother Jane Withers. 'Now Don looks like Ron and Ron looks like Don. Hopefully now they can both start a completely new life with their entirely new look.'

For the past three years Mrs Withers has fought a lone battle against the National Health Service who consistently refused to carry out the radical and very expensive operation on her two identical sons. 'The bureaucrats and accountants in the NHS just didn't want to know,' said Mrs Withers. 'One doctor even said, "What's the point?" Like there's one rule for identical twins and another rule for everybody else!'

But luckily for the Withers family, a little-known Russian surgeon had read about her plight and offered to carry out the operation privately. 'I couldn't believe my luck when Mr Yarov said he would be prepared to do the transplant if I could raise the necessary cash. Some people might think that half a million pounds is a lot of money for a face swap, but my two boys are worth it.'

Ron and Don Withers were then taken to Mr Yarov's impromptu operating theatre where they were given a general anaesthetic. Many hours later they awoke, wrapped in bandages, with their anxious mother sitting beside them awaiting the finished result. 'I hadn't been allowed to see the operating theatre, or meet any of the other medical staff involved because of health and safety regulations. But when Mr Yarov took off the bandages I couldn't believe my eyes. My boys looked perfect – not a bruise or a scar on them; you'd never think that they'd just been through a major op! I've had to sell my house and cash in my pension, but Mr Yarov deserves every penny if this can help my two boys start a new life.'

Nostradamus 'predicted squeezy Marmite jars'

9 June

A new study published today claims that the sixteenth-century soothsayer Nostradamus predicted the revolutionary new squeezy Marmite jar.

The convenient yeast-spread serving solution was only launched a couple of years ago and yet it appears that its invention was foreseen nearly four hundred years ago by the great Renaissance prophet.

'This is an incredibly exciting discovery in one of the world's most famous texts,' said Kenneth Jupp from the Nostradamus Society. 'We know that Michel de Nostredame foresaw the rise of Hitler and Napoleon, the assassination of Kennedy and the nuclear bomb. But there was one section that made no sense. That's because it hadn't happened until now!'

For years scholars had been baffled by quatrains 56 and 57, hypothesizing about possible references to the beheading of Charles I or the Great Fire of London. But with this new translation from the old French it has suddenly become clear that the baffling verses refer to the popular savoury spread and the problems of extracting the last bit from the jar:

> And the Angles shall season their crust with salty yeast,
> Thick but thin, it shall bring love or hate,
> But the tub shall hide the final share,
> And men shall weep and curse the elusive tub.
>
> And so the pot shall be o'er-turned,
> And glass shall be no more,
> And men shall grasp the yielding gourd,
> But you still won't be able to get the last
> bit, though it's fun drawing faces on your toast.

The British Library, however, has questioned the accuracy of this new edition of the prophecies, suggesting that Marmite's PR company have been very liberal with their translation of the original French.

CANCER VICTIM WAS NEITHER BRAVE NOR WELL LIKED

11 June

Family and friends of 37-year-old Jez Coddington, who passed away at the weekend following a brief battle with cancer, spoke last night of their indifference at losing someone they thought of as 'OK'.

Jez's 'best friend' Dave Fothergill confessed to being 'not that bothered' by the loss, saying, 'I'd known Jez since primary school, but we haven't really had that much in common for years. I was interested in football, novels, films and stuff, but he was mostly just into Warhammer and internet porn. He was always a bit embarrassing, but when you've known someone that long, it's hard to tell them you don't want to hang around with them any more.'

Jez's girlfriend Jennifer expressed similar sentiments: 'I thought I'd be more upset about it, but it's a bit of a relief, to be honest. I actually thought he was a little bit creepy. We hadn't been going out all that long when he was diagnosed, and I couldn't really leave him after that, no matter how much of a pain in the arse he was.'

It is understood that Jez did not deal with his illness in the courageous and inspirational manner demonstrated by celebrities like Roy Castle or Kylie Minogue. 'He was boring before the illness, and this just gave him something else to be boring about,' said Jennifer, speaking from the flat of her new boyfriend. 'I mean, cancer's no picnic, I'm sure. But it just made him even more selfish than before. "Oooh I'm ill: make me a sandwich, buy me a Playstation, fetch my porn magazines from under the mattress." '

In the light of the comments from Jez's 'friends' and family, the vicar giving the eulogy at his funeral has cut out all former references to Jez's heroism and good humour in the face of the killer disease. 'He didn't have to do that,' said Jez's former girlfriend. 'I mean, no one's going to be there anyway.'

SECOND SAT NAV ARGUES ABOUT BEST ROUTE

14 June

The satellite-navigation revolution suffered a setback this week as a new report claimed husbands in the passenger seat are buying their own Sat Navs to disagree with the one their wives are listening to.

Audio satellite navigation had promised to stop the endless arguments about the best route that have plagued married couples since the invention of the motor car. But it seems that the technological breakthrough has only led to another means by which couples can argue. Last week the children of the Thomson family from Bristol sat in awkward silence in the back seat while the electronic voices belonging to their parents' two Sat Navs argued it out in the front:

'At the next junction, turn left.'
'No, don't turn left, that's a stupid route.'
'Don't fucking tell me which route to take.'
'Don't use that sort of language with me. No one wants to go to your fucking mother's anyway.'

The marriage-guidance service Relate have recommended that all couples take their second satellite-navigation system back to the shop. Mr and Mrs Thomson, however, filed for divorce this weekend after failing to agree on the best route back to Halfords.

Traffic lights to have four colours

15 June

Following concerns about the increasing complexity of traffic junctions, the Ministry of Transport has announced that, as from next year, the traditional three traffic-light colours of red, amber and green will be joined by an additional colour: blue.

'The three colours were fine when it was a simple case of stop, get ready, go!' said Junior Transport Minister Keith Pinder MP. 'But this new light brings more possibilities at our increasingly busy traffic junctions.'

According to the minister's official statement, the Highway Code will now recommend the following responses at light-controlled junctions. Red: stop! Amber: stop, unless it would cause an accident to do so. Green: proceed with caution. Blue: edge forward looking confused; realize that you shouldn't be in the little yellow box; panic; reverse without looking; break headlights of car behind.

'If blue comes after amber, it signifies 'check mirror for police cars, accelerate through changing light, swerve to avoid swearing cyclist,' continued Pinder. 'However, if blue appears at the same time as red, amber and green, it means you have been eating magic mushrooms and should not be in control of a motor vehicle.'

'For pedestrians there will also be additional figures. As well as the little red man standing still and the green man crossing the road, there will be a little purple man darting between the stationary traffic and then nearly getting knocked down by a moped delivering pizza.'

To the surprise of the journalists who had attended the press conference, the minister then read the final paragraph from the official statement that had been prepared by one of his civil servants: 'By the way, this is all complete bollocks, but I knew he'd just read it out. In future, Keith, do not attempt to grope me in the stationery cupboard; I am not your bitch.'

The government denied that the whole announcement was an embarrassing mistake and are pressing ahead with the new lights next year.

Thailand suffers wave of 'petty-crime tourists'

16 June

British men hoping to avoid the shame and embarrassment that committing petty crimes would bring at home are flying in their thousands to Thailand where they can indulge in minor civil offences without anyone at home finding out.

YOUTUBE TURNS DOWN SECOND SEASON OF JOEY

18 June

Friends spin-off *Joey* has hit another stumbling block in its efforts to attract potential broadcasters after it was repeatedly refused broadcasting space on video-sharing website YouTube.

The show, starring Matt LeBlanc, showed early promise with audiences for the first season starting at four million, but these dropped to under five hundred thousand after episode four and then fell to just twelve after NBC moved its slot to 2.45 a.m. on Tuesdays.

NBC have shown no interest in airing the second season but LeBlanc has financed, filmed and edited the thirty-six-episode new series in anticipation that the show would find a network sooner or later.

'It has been a bit of a setback, '

LeBlanc explained, 'but after HBO, Fox, S4C and al-Jazeera 2 told us "thanks, but no thanks" I truly believed that we could find a suitable outlet online. Sadly, whenever I try and upload the shows in two-minute sections, they are removed by moderators within seconds and so we have had to finally admit that the dream may be over.'

LeBlanc's disappointment was not made any easier by television executives regularly showing him the ratings graph and saying, 'How YOU doin'?'

A new report published this week has revealed a shocking catalogue of petty crimes being committed by outwardly respectable British men who regularly visit the back streets of Bangkok for the illicit thrill of parking on double yellow lines, cycling on the pavement and crossing the road when the little red man is showing.

One such petty-crime tourist is 'Ken' from Daventry (not his real name): 'If the people at work knew

what I did during my week off they'd be appalled. But when I come out here I can indulge my darkest fantasies: downloading free songs off the internet, leaving shopping trolleys in the multi-storey car park and taking clothes back to Marks and Spencer after I've worn them a couple of times.'

It's not just British men who head to Asia to get their kicks from technical law-breaking. One elderly

German man disappeared up a narrow stairway that promised discreet 'home-taping'. A large Dutchman claimed he came here every year to buy a beer from one bar, and walk with the half-full glass on to the next one. But these are not victimless crimes. Each year hundreds of young women are driven in from rural areas in cars with defective rear seatbelts. Girls as young as fourteen were being taken to see films with a 15 certificate.

Now the new Thai government is clamping down on petty-crime tourists by posting their photos on the internet. 'That's me there,' said 'Ken' from Daventry, using the unsecured wireless network of the hotel next door without their permission.

James Bond 'disappointed with only an MBE'

British secret agent James Bond is reported to be 'privately a little disappointed' that official recognition of his services to his country apparently amounts only to an MBE.

19 June

The heroic spy's name was put forward in recognition of 'services to British intelligence' and, as is customary, the various nominees were contacted well in advance of the Queen's birthday to check that they would in fact accept an honour.

But on receipt of the letter Mr Bond was reported to have lost his temper. 'Frankly, after all the shit I've been through, you'd think a bloody peerage would be the absolute minimum,' Bond apparently shouted at Miss Moneypenny, who had excitedly showed him the letter. 'An MBE is like the worst one of all of them, isn't it? I mean that Jimmy Savile's got an OBE and a knighthood, but I'm apparently not as good as a creepy senile radio presenter.'

Miss Moneypenny attempted to mollify 007 with suggestions that if he continued to save the world from crazed criminal geniuses then he might get promoted to a CBE later in his career, but this seemingly did little to diminish Mr Bond's anger. 'You lay your life on the line, time and time again, you defeat private armies and switch off nuclear detonators with only seconds to spare, and what does that get you? "Member of the British Empire . . ." Spiffing. My name is Bond, James Bond MBE. On a par with Michael bloody Fish and Alan Titchmarsh.'

Women's tennis; stalkers to be seeded

20 June

The All England Lawn Tennis Club has finally agreed to formalize the ranking of stalkers of female tennis players.

Up until now the distribution of obsessive and dangerous male fans had been somewhat chaotic, with certain tennis stars having several stalkers and others having none.

The new stalker seeding system will allow a fairer spread of restraining orders, an equal number of aggressive letters proposing marriage and a guarantee that the entertainment of security guards wrestling nutters to the ground will be spread over the entire Wimbledon fortnight. The most crazed and possessive schizophrenics will be allocated to the top female tennis players. Middle-ranking players will become aware that the same creepy man is always outside their hotel window, while England's number-one female tennis star will just have a kindly old gentleman who sends her a Christmas card every year.

BRITAIN'S YOUTH SEIZED BY CRAZE FOR INTERNAL BODY PIERCING

21 June

Trendsetters in Britain's inner cities are leading the way with the latest fashion craze to grip the nation's youth culture: internal body piercing.

Over the past couple of decades, nose studs, pierced tongues and rings through the eyebrow have become a common sight. But now the fad has gone a stage further as young people are paying surgeons to have piercings inserted through their internal organs.

Twenty-two-year-old 'Zed', who works part-time in a snowboard and surfing shop, already has a gold ring in his pancreas and a diamond in his bile duct. But last weekend he underwent a two-hour operation to have a silver-plated stud put into his spleen.

'It costs a few bob, but it's worth it,' said Zed. 'Having a stud in your spleen isn't just about being cool. It also really heightens the pleasure of having your red blood cells refined.'

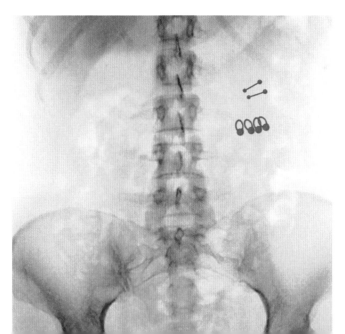

Robots 'have failed to take over the world'

Predictions that robots and computers would rise up and enslave mankind have turned out to be completely wrong, admitted a veteran science-fiction writer yesterday.

22 June

'We were convinced that with all this technology and computers and everything, pretty soon humans would be like the slaves and computerized robots would be like the masters . . . ' said Lee Duxbury to his shame-faced audience at an SF conference in Toronto.

'My chilling cult novel *Planet Silicon 2000* depicted a fascist robot government publicly executing human freedom fighters for daring to challenge the android master-race. (Except Xena, the beautiful but conflicted half-human, half-robot who eventually joins forces with the rebels after falling in love with the hero Cal.) But let's face it – none of it has come true. This weekend my Sat Nav instructed me to take a left when I wanted to take a right, but it turned out I was wrong and the machine was correct. It was actually really helpful.'

Another speaker proposed a formal apology from the Association of Science Fiction Writers: 'We said that the machines would rise up, that it would be the computers giving the orders to us. But the worst that has happened is that a little paperclip pops up on Microsoft Word to help you lay out your letter. How nightmarish and totalitarian is that? We should be ashamed of ourselves.'

At this point the SF conference was dramatically broken up after a delegate leapt to the stage and grabbed the keynote speaker, attempting to find some sort of metal casing at the back of his head in order to pull out all his wires. The delegate was embarrassed to discover, however, that he was just an ordinary person like everyone else.

FRANCE TO BE 'CONSTANTLY REMINDED' IT LOST 2012 OLYMPICS

23 June

Plans for the London Olympics in 2012 are being revised as concerns grow that the French are forgetting the former favourites to win the games were beaten by London.

Lord Coe, who led Britain's successful Olympic bid, said, 'In a few years' time, when all the athletes are competing in the 2012 games, no one will remember how devastated the French were to lose out to the English. So it will be our job to keep reminding them.'

The official title for the games will be 'The 2012 London (not Paris) Olympics'. Videos of the moment the French delegation learnt of their defeat will be endlessly played in the Olympic Village, while the opening ceremony will feature hundreds of London schoolchildren running into the stadium, releasing doves of peace and then kicking a cartoon Frenchman up the arse.

'We want these games to be different,' said Lord Coe. 'It's not about the sporting ideal, nor about different nations coming together. It's about really pissing off the French.'

GARY GLITTER MUSICAL FAILS TO FIND INVESTORS 24 June

Following the success of *Mamma Mia*, *We Will Rock You* and a host of nostalgic West End musicals, would-be theatrical impresario Cliff Powell had been confident that there was another hit show just waiting in the wings.

However, the main investor in the new Gary Glitter musical *My Gang!* today announced that the show now looks unlikely to happen. Mr Powell, who has given years of his life to this project, said, 'We contacted hundreds of potential investors with the message "Do You Wanna Be in My Gang?" and quite a strong signal came back saying, "Well, no."'

Back in the seventies Gary Glitter topped the charts with hits such as 'Do You Wanna Touch Me', 'I'm the Leader of the Gang (I Am)' and 'I Love You Love Me Love'.

However, the former glam-rock star has recently been the subject of some negative publicity, which Cliff Powell conceded may have made financial backers a little wary that his family show had a future. 'Why can't people just enjoy the music?' he complained. 'It's just political correctness gone mad.'

Four horsemen of the Apocalypse split; 'Pestilence to go solo' 25 June

A spokesman for the legendary Horsemen of the Apocalypse has confirmed rumours that the famous foursome are to split over 'apocalyptic differences' following a statement from Pestilence that he intended to concentrate on his solo career.

'Pestilence has had a great time with the guys over the past few millennia, but feels that the time has come to move on,' said his manager to shocked journalists.

However, conflicting rumours are circulating the underworld which suggest that Pestilence may have actually been thrown out by the other three, who have been hinting for some time that they felt they were carrying him. The remaining horsemen have not yet confirmed whether they will continue to tour as a threesome or also take some time out to develop solo projects. Despite having remained unchanged for thousands of years, the famous line-up had continued touring Africa, parts of Asia and the Middle East and had been planning American and European tours 'in the near future'.

'We don't need Pestilence – he brought nothing to the band,' said War in a recent interview. 'Every time we talked about trashing some country, he was always like, "and then maybe a load of locusts fly in and eat all the wheat?" Like, please? Has he not heard of pesticides? It's over, Pestilence! Accept it.'

However, other sources blame War, himself for the split. 'It all started when War let his horse-mad girlfriend tag along,' claims one fan. 'He started to say that Samantha had got some really interesting ideas about changing their image, putting less emphasis on Apocalypses and more on Gymkhanas and Show Jumping . . .'

Bitter exchanges have continued to fly back and forth between the two camps. Pestilence was reported to be in Southern India where a plague of Colorado beetles devastated a local potato crop, while the other three horsemen were spotted at the Windsor Horse trials where Famine won a rosette in the dressage section.

Cerne Abbas – giant penis was added by 12-year-old boys

26 June

Archaeologists have discovered evidence that the giant penis on the famous Iron Age chalk carving in Dorset was added by a pair of twelve-year-old boys who subsequently found themselves in a lot of trouble.

For centuries historians have debated the significance of the ancient Cerne Abbas giant. Many believe that the enormous erect penis must symbolize a pagan fertility god, or perhaps an ancestral warrior or hero. But ancient runes discovered near the site have finally revealed the truth – that the big erection was added on by two Iron Age adolescent boys for a prank.

In fact, the original carving was of a much-respected village elder, and druids and warriors from miles around were summoned to admire the dignified image. But on the morning of the festival, the village awoke to see that the venerated chief had had a great big erect penis added on. The ancient runes end with an account of how the boys were chastised by their Iron Age elders: 'You haven't just let yourselves down,' the head druid told them. 'You've let your parents down, you've let me down and you've let this whole Iron Age community down.'

ROSA PARKS 'WAS VICTIM OF SUPERGLUE PRANK'

27 June

Civil rights leaders in America have admitted that Rosa Parks, the black woman who famously refused to vacate her seat on the bus for a white man, was not quite as much of a heroine as was previously thought.

Montgomery County files, released yesterday after their classified status elapsed, have revealed that she was actually physically unable to get up after being superglued to the chair.

Sgt. Bill Huckey of Montgomery County Police said, 'The record needs to be set straight. Us cops have been painted as the bad guys. When the bus driver told her to give up her seat she tried, but it was impossible.' History shows that it took three policemen to physically remove Ms Parks from the bus, but Huckey claimed that 'we'd no way to dissolve the glue, it was brute force or nothing'.

The superglue had actually been placed on the seat by her mischievous nephews as a prank, who had no idea that the whole thing would precipitate a civil rights campaign, the mobilization of the National Guard and the end to legal segregation. Black civil rights leaders were quick to make her a heroine and a focus for the movement, and she was happy to accept the fiction of her dignified protest if it stopped her nephews getting into trouble. However, after a while some civil rights leaders, notably Martin Luther King Jnr, did accuse her of 'milking it a bit'. 'She didn't even use the bus as a general rule,' said one, adding that Rosa was a bit of a 'one-hit wonder' and that 'her later work lacked the same impact'.

POLICE STAB HEROIN NEEDLE INTO WRONG MAN

28 June

A pilot scheme being run by the Metropolitan Police in which drug addicts are prescribed heroin in order to reduce crime backfired yesterday when an innocent man was repeatedly injected by police officers.

The incident occurred at Oval underground station in south London, where, according to the police version of events, the suspicious-looking man approached the officers concerned exposing his forearm and tightening a tourniquet as he said, 'I am a drug addict, give me my smack or I'll commit lots of crimes.'

However, independent witnesses have told a very different story. They describe the victim as an ordinary commuter who had just picked up a free newspaper and swiped his Oyster card. 'Suddenly five policemen jumped on him, wrestled him to the ground and repeatedly stabbed him using semi-automatic syringes,' said a passer-by. 'They shouted "Take that, smackhead!" and even when he was completely spaced out and obviously really high, they just kept pumping more and more heroin into him.'

Met Commissioner Sir Ian Blair defended his officers in the front line of the war on drugs and crime: 'Our policemen only have a split second to decide if someone is a potential heroin addict or not. If we do not act quickly, that drug addict may wander up to some passengers and ask them for money or go and try and get the coins out of parking meters.'

The victim, an IT consultant who has never been in trouble with the police, later regained consciousness and was reported to be overwhelmed with a need to get another massive dose of heroin. He was last seen robbing someone at knifepoint in order to pay for his new habit.

Banks 'testing financial services on animals'

29 June

Animal-rights campaigners vowed a 'swift and brutal' campaign of retaliation today after it emerged that several high street banks have been testing their services on animals.

The banks, who have all previously denied that they are involved in vivisection, have arranged extra security measures to counter the threat from the Animal Liberation Front, who said that 'every employee, every branch, and every person linked to the banks concerned is a valid target, and will probably have their tyres slashed and nasty graffiti sprayed on their house.'

The news broke when a whistle-blower from Lloyds claimed that animals were routinely used to determine the sales potential of a range of financial arrangements, ranging from mortgages to mini ISAs. Clare Stafford, a former member of the Lloyds Insurance and Investment team, declared in a statement: 'Some of the scenes were really horrific. They would put a monkey in a room and make him choose between two different mortgage deals: a fixed-rate deal and a standard variable rate, for example. Then they'd force him to choose between a variety of loans, each for different amounts and with different rates of interest. And then at the end of the day they'd put him back in his cage and give him a banana, as if that compensated for all the traumatic financial decisions he had had to make. It was so upsetting.'

She also alleged that the banks attempted to convince the monkeys to purchase insurance, and in extreme cases even repossessed their cages if they got themselves into debt through poor decision-making.

A member of the ALF said that their retribution would be typically swift, unpleasant, and entirely justified. 'It is barbaric that in this day and age innocent monkeys can be subjected to this kind of torture, without any concern for the horrendous effects it has on their credit rating. These monkeys will never be able to take out a student loan, buy a house or start up a business, and we see it as our duty to find who is responsible for this torture and to dig up their grandparents' graves. It's the only reasonable response.'

TOUGH DRAW FOR ENGLISH IN TERRORISM WORLD CUP

30 June

The Animal Liberation Front, who are representing England in next year's Terrorism World Cup, have been drawn into what is generally considered the toughest qualifying group.

Group B, the so-called 'Group of Death', pits the plucky animal-lovers from England against al-Qaeda, the Shining Path of Peru and the Baader-Meinhof gang. 'Although the Germans are not the force they once were . . . ' commente John Motson at the draw, 'being as they are without Baade Or indeed Meinhof.'

There is also the prospect of an interesting local derby: Continuity IRA have been drawn against the Ulster Volunteer Force, which has historically been a very niggly fixture. The end of the draw was disrupted when, instead of pulling a little numbered ball out of the bag, one of the officials drew out a large black fizzing ball with 'BOMB'

written on one side. 'How disappointing,' added John Motson. 'And you have to say, that's just the sort of behaviour that gives terrorism a bad name.'

'Alternative Shaving Centre' unable to explain long beards

1 July

A so-called 'Alternative Shaving Centre' that has been charging patients thousands of pounds to unlock holistic, non-interventionist methods of removing facial hair has been accused of extortion after all of its residents were photographed with very long beards.

'Those are just the natural toxins coming out,' said the centre's founder Dave Cunliffe. 'These things take time. But eventually our residents will learn to cure themselves of unwanted hair growth the spiritual way, without the harsh intervention of metal blades or electric shavers. They will be clean shaven through the power of their own minds,' he explained. 'We see facial hair as a symptom of an imbalance in the body's energy field.'

But former visitors to the Alternative Shaving Centre in rural Sussex claim that they paid thousands of pounds to meditate and chant and wave crystals over their chins with no visible change in the rate of hair growth.

'I actually came out of the centre with a little goatee beard and I'd never had a facial hair problem before I went in,' said mother-of-two Alison Welling. 'I was only working there as an administrator.'

'Not everyone is able to locate their inner stubble,' explained natural shaving guru Dave Cunliffe, who denies accusations that he himself has been seen using a Gillette Mach II wet razor while his patients were supposed to have their eyes closed during chanting led by the self-styled yogic barber. 'OK, that guy who complained never managed to stop his beard growing. He is going bald though, so that proves it sort of works.'

2 July

With life in the countryside becoming increasingly difficult, a number of farmers have been migrating to the cities, where they can now be spotted at night, disappearing behind advertising hoardings or making temporary homes on bits of waste land.

Inner cities being over-run by 'urban farmers'

'We've had an urban farmer and his family living behind our garden shed all winter,' said Mrs Dalton of Kennington, London. 'There was the farmer, his wife, two grown-up sons and about three hundred dairy cattle. It made a right mess of the flowerbeds.'

Other city-dwellers have complained of the noise the urban farmers make in the small hours. 'In the middle of the night you'll suddenly hear them scampering about, planting winter cabbage and driving tractors around the waste ground next door,' said another local resident. 'They're bloody pests. I came down in the morning and all the plants in my

Iraq persuaded to purchase extended warranty

5 July

United States forces withdrawing from Baghdad have managed to persuade the new Iraqi government to pay for an expensive extended-warranty agreement that provides limited labour and parts cover for the fragile democracy that was set up under the allies.

'Although we are confident that the Iraqis will enjoy years of trouble-free satisfaction from their new representative form of government, it is always worth insuring against the possibility that something could go wrong,' explained Condoleezza Rice. 'This extra cover gives them the confidence to enjoy their new Freedom™ with complete peace of mind.'

For just an extra forty billion dollars, Iraq can rest assured that if their new pro-Western government should go wrong in any way, then one of the after-care team can be called out using the exclusive warranty helpline. 'Of course we're not talking about sending in ground forces all over again,' explained Ms Rice. 'But bombs will be made available, delivered by air within twenty-four hours of the first call to a central Baghdad location.'

Iraqi ministers complained, however, that on testing the helpline, a recorded voice offered them a range of unappealing choices and then put them on hold for ages while they were forced to listen to *Boléro*: 'If you wish to destabilize a neighbour, press one. If you wish to be added to the Axis of Evil, press two. If you wish to order a nuclear air strike, precipitating the outbreak of World War Three, press the hache key now.'

garden had been harvested and wrapped up in a big black bin liner.'

Now there are calls to cull these so-called 'pests' to prevent them causing any more havoc and expense. But other residents welcome these visitors from the countryside and leave out little treats for them at night, like large EU subsidies and unfashionable clothing. 'I think they are sweet,' said Marjorie Simmonds of Bristol. 'They bring a little bit of the country to the urban back garden. Although I'm not allowed on my lawn any more. Not since they fenced it off and put up big signs saying "Keep Out".'

Britney Spears to be adopted by African child

7 July

The family of Arthur Zimba, an eight-year-old Malawian boy, have asked for privacy as they help his recently adopted sister, Britney Spears, settle into her new life in their village, far away from the dangers of her LA lifestyle.

Arthur asked his parents if he could adopt the troubled superstar after her latest cry for help saw her admitted to a psychiatric hospital in California. 'Some people watch the showbiz news and sigh, "What can we do . . ?"' said Arthur. 'But I believe if I, as a poor African child, can make a difference to just one celebrity's life I have a moral duty to do something.'

For the Zimbas, taking the former child-star under the corrugated iron roof of their mud-hut home is the culmination of years spent watching news stories about suffering Hollywood celebrities, who often end up in trouble with the law for shoplifting or kerb-crawling, or addicted to drugs and prescription medication.

'And the deprivation!' remarked Arthur's mother. 'These Hollywood starlets clearly don't even have the money to buy a pair of knickers. And they are so stick-like; they're obviously being starved.'

Questions have been raised about how the Zimbas were able to rush through the Britney adoption and the fact that the judge on the case was subsequently offered her own chat-show and magazine deals. 'I can see how that might look suspicious to you or me,' explained Arthur's father Yohane, 'but that's just the way things are done over there.'

The future should be bright now for Britney, with a steady job in one of Malawi's growing industries, which could even see her working for Disney once again – only this time as a seamstress producing the latest line of Mickey Mouse Club merchandise.

Champion shot-putter depressed at no practical use for talent

8 July

Olympic shot-putter Geoff Pike is reported to be seriously depressed after coming to the conclusion that there is no practical use for his extraordinary shot-putting ability.

Pike became something of a British sporting hero after he won the Olympic Silver Medal in the shot-put back at the 2008 Beijing Olympics. However, he told reporters this week from his home in Cheadle, 'What's the point? If you are a champion runner at least you can always catch a bus. A weightlifter can carry loads of stuff from the car into his house. But when does anyone ever need to hurl a very heavy metal ball from under their chin to the near distance? Why did I have to be good at that? My whole life has been a complete waste of time.'

Pike is now reported to have taken up the piano, although he is apparently frustrated that, unlike with shot-putting, he seems to have no natural ability in this area whatsoever.

Dramatic increase in the number of proud parents whose sons 'do something with computers'

9 July

The government has been criticized for cutting the number of staff working for the British Jobs Survey, and relying instead on information gathered from the elderly parents of those in work.

The latest figures based on this method of collecting employment data have seen a dramatic rise in the number of people who 'do something in computers' with the encouraging news that 100 per cent of them 'are doing very well'. Other jobs that were revealed to be on the increase were 'working in London', 'something to do with money' and 'in a very smart office'. According to the survey of parents, not a single individual was reported to be working as a 'senior financial adviser to systems analyst set-ups', although this may have been covered by the wider demographic described as 'working for a big firm who are one of the top ones'.

'It is ridiculous to attempt to rely on this sort of vague and ill-informed data,' said Professor Sally-Anne Donohue, Senior Statistician at the British Jobs Survey. However, her authority to comment on such matters was brought into question by her official entry in the Elderly Parents' Survey. According to the latest information: 'Sally-Anne's still working at the moment, yes, which is a shame. I think she's a secretary or something. But these days it's actually quite common for a girl to work for a little while before she starts a family. I expect she'll meet a nice man soon and be able to stay at home. Our Bryan's doing very well though. He's something to do with computers . . .'

Accommodation shortages as bees opt to live alone

15 July

Britain is facing a major shortage of bee hives as modern, younger bees are choosing to reject traditional communal living and are opting instead for the freedom and independence that comes from living on their own.

'It's been getting worse every year,' said apiarist Mike Chatterton from Devon, who has been keeping bees for forty years. 'In the old days, you'd put a hive in your back garden and around thirty thousand busy-busy bees would soon settle in it. Now they've decided they'd like things a little quieter. It only takes one bee to move in, and then another one comes along and thinks, Oh, I don't want to live there – there's another bee already in residence.'

Modern hive construction has attempted to accommodate the social change in the living choices of bees, with high-rise 'bee flats' replacing the crowded, shared honeycomb that bees have endured down the centuries, but even these are now being rejected: 'The bees don't just want their own little hive, they want a balcony, a small garden and a bit of personal space to fly around in.'

Many bees continue to produce honey in the smaller personalized hives, but the extraction process is inefficient and time-consuming. 'Though not all bees are content to be told that all they are going to do is produce honey for the rest of their lives,' explains Mike Chatterton. 'Some of the younger ones want a gap year, or to travel. Oh, and when they come back they've decided they want to be a wasp.'

Prince Harry 'to be normal ex-soldier' and live on streets

17 July

Prince Harry's plan to be just like any other soldier returning from a tour of duty were under review today when it was revealed he is now sleeping on the streets and begging for cash towards his next bottle of cooking sherry.

After finding his family and friends difficult to relate to on his return from Afghanistan, the Prince lasted just one night holding down a part-time job as a nightclub bouncer. Having married a childhood sweetheart called Chelsy in haste, he immediately decided it was a big mistake and walked out on her and the kids before seeking solace in alcohol. The homeless Prince soon began to suffer anxiety attacks and nightmares as he relived his wartime experiences. With limited access to psychological support he has already developed full-blown post-traumatic stress disorder.

'I think it's marvellous that the Prince is not getting any special

WAR VETERAN.
PLEASE GIVE
OODLES OF CASH.

treatment' said on government defence minister; 'We can all be enormously proud that he is out there just like any other squaddie, sleeping in doorways, growing increasingly bitter and wondering how he might use his firearms expertise to express his hatred for mainstream society.

Some cynics have suggested that the whole episode has been a PR stunt to show the Prince as a regular guy and that now that his whereabouts have been revealed, Prince Harry has an excuse to return to Buckingham Palace. Whatever happens, the Prince has shown that he can hack it like the rest of his regiment,' said his former commander. 'In fact he took to it better than many of the others. Taking handouts and appearing drunk in public just seemed to come to him naturally . . .'

McDonald's launches 'fat patches' for lazy eaters

18 July

HIGH-STREET FAST-FOOD CHAIN MCDONALD'S TODAY LAUNCHED A NEW RANGE OF 'FAT PATCHES' FOR PEOPLE WHO CAN'T BE BOTHERED TO WALK ALL THE WAY TO THEIR LOCAL RESTAURANT.

The new patches release 100 per cent saturated fats and additives, and allow the wearer to enjoy the complete McDonald's experience without leaving the comfort of their armchair or hoist.

Eileen Mahoney, 23 stone, said, 'Before these wonder patches were available I had to get dressed, have a shave and walk two hundred yards to my local burger outlet where I would order forty-five chicken nuggets, eight portions of fries, six milkshakes and five McFlurries for breakfast. Even going to the Drive-In Burger King meant walking to the car. Now I simply reach across to the fridge next to my armchair and unwrap a giant fat patch – it contains the same amount of transfats, modified starch and artificial sweeteners, without all that effort!'

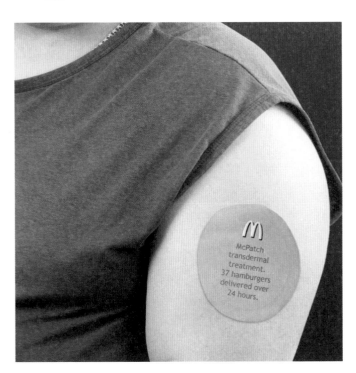

McPatch
transdermal
treatment.
37 hamburgers
delivered over
24 hours.

Other fast-food outlets are said to be watching the latest development with interest. A spokesman for KFC said, 'This will not affect plans for our new "fat-laden chicken lardy-bucket by post" initiative which we are launching in partnership with Amazon in an effort to deliver delicious fried chicken soaked in transfats with extra salt to buyers within eight days of ordering.'

GLASTONBURY MAN CLAIMS ALIENS CREATED 'ROAD CIRCLES'

20 July

A Glastonbury man has claimed that the sudden appearance of what he calls 'road circles' are the work of alien visitors to Planet Earth. Mr Philip Brun, who runs a new-age bookshop and alternative healing centre, says that there is no other logical reason for why a normal crossroads should suddenly be mysteriously replaced with the highly symbolic road shape.

Summoning journalists to the scene for a press conference, Mr Brun defied the assembled witnesses to come up with any other explanation for the 'road circle' they saw before them.

'It's a mini-roundabout,' sighed one reporter.

'Call it what you will. But when viewed from up in the sky, these beacons appear as perfect circles. Who else could have put them there but aliens from outer space?'

'How about the local council?'

'Oh yeah, right!' Mr Brun scoffed. 'And I suppose that explains all the other road circles that have appeared all over the country, does it?'

'Yes. The local authority or the Highways Agency regularly put in mini-roundabouts to ease traffic flow at busy road junctions.'

Mr Brun went quiet for a moment and then attempted to claim he had actually seen the aliens putting in the road circles and that they were green and spoke a strange language. On further questioning it transpired that only their safety jackets were green, and that the language was Polish.

Google launches 'YouSnoop'

YouSnoop

22 July

Google today launched a handy new facility which allows browsers to observe the private lives of any other computer user.

Google 'YouSnoop' seamlessly combines YouTube, its recently acquired video posting website, with Google Earth, Google Mail and Picasa to reveal images, personal correspondence and much more about unsuspecting strangers.

'You just double-click the spyglass icon which will appear on YouSnoop and Google Earth will open up and spin round to the exact home you are searching for,' says Google founder Sergey Brin. 'Say you want to know what that perfect family from church get up to behind closed doors: you just enter basic details into the YouSnoop search box, and suddenly you can watch them live on your monitor and access all the information on their personal computers. It's really neat.'

Clicking on the mug icon brings up the subject's name, a picture, personal emails, bank-account details, links to favourite pornography websites, and what they said about themselves on discreet online adult 'friend-finder' sites.

Google expects a huge revenue stream from YouSnoop and the company's shares rose another 2 per cent on news of the launch. Millions of people have already signed up for the service, eagerly entering a long list of personal details to gain access. Users are already enjoying laughing at the embarrassing behaviour of others, leaving comments about appalling décor or dodgy underwear. A surprising number of people are also spending hours watching themselves to see if they get up to anything. However, once they find out what Google has on them they generally want it hidden pretty quickly. To get that done, users are offered the opportunity to subscribe to a new service called 'Google Blackmail'.

Sofaland declares independence from Kingdom of Leather

24 July

THE UNITED NATIONS MET IN EMERGENCY SESSION TODAY FOLLOWING THE SHOCK NEWS THAT SOFALAND HAD UNILATERALLY BROKEN AWAY FROM ITS HISTORIC RULERS, THE KINGDOM OF LEATHER.

The leather superpower has refused to recognize the separatist soft-furnishing republic, and has called on the UN to protect the vulnerable leather-sofa minority that wish to remain part of the disintegrating kingdom. But without the crucial support of Curtain Kingdom, which holds the balance of power in the region, Sofaland may struggle to hold on to its own ethnic cushion community, which itself is looking for autonomy.

The United Nations already has troops in the region, following last year's break-up of Furnitureland, and there are fears that British forces may have to be redeployed away from their peace-keeping duties in Pine Village and CarpetCity. But soft-furnishing torture has still not yet been fully stamped out by the occupying forces, with one recent report of a carpet being stretched out and nailed to the floor, while a range of curtains was discovered hanging in a showroom in a nearby retail park. 'They look as if they've been ruffed up,' said a British officer.

As the crisis deepens, World of Beds has offered asylum to fleeing sofa-beds who have until now been forced to hide their bed-like heritage. 'We have no historic homeland,' said a spokesman for the oppressed sofa-bed community. 'We are part sofa, part bed; it is time for the politicians to sit down and sort this out. Or lie down. We can't decide.'

David Blaine in gruelling attempt to watch his own stunts

27 July

Internationally renowned street magician David Blaine today officially announced his new performance stunt. David will be locked in a room and forced to watch the DVDs of all his previous stunts, back to back, twenty-four hours a day, for a full week.

Doctors have expressed concern that David is at risk of being 'bored to death' by watching himself for such a prolonged period, but Blaine believes he can survive the ordeal.

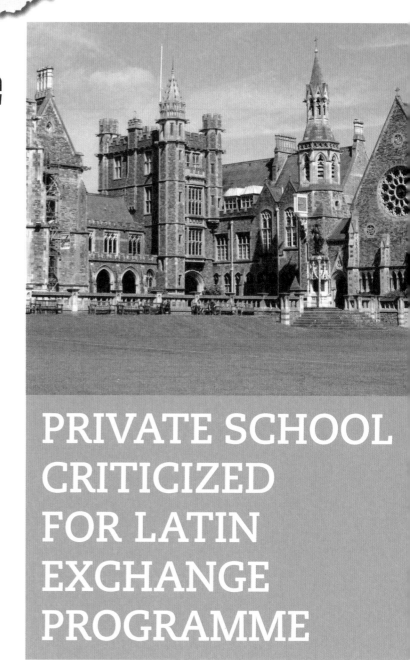

PRIVATE SCHOOL CRITICIZED FOR LATIN EXCHANGE PROGRAMME

30 July

One of Britain's top private schools has come under fire after launching a Latin exchange programme for its pupils.

Spencer House College in Hampshire is one of the most exclusive boarding schools in the country, but has provoked anxiety among parents whose children are currently taking part in the first residential school trips to 'Ancient Rome'.

'Nothing improves a child's facility in a language more than immersing himself in that society and culture,' explained Clive Stafford MA, Head of Classics at Spencer House. 'Latin scholars have always been at a disadvantage compared to the students of modern foreign languages. But now our boys can spend two weeks speaking Latin all day every day, and really get to understand what it felt like to be an ancient Briton in the Roman Empire.'

With no one having spoken Latin for over a thousand years, the Roman environment has had to be artificially recreated at a villa in Central Italy. The families, made up of Latin-speaking actors, are under strict instructions to stick to Roman customs and traditions at all times. They eat olives wrapped in larks' tongues and then go to the vomitorium to regurgitate them again.

'My Timmy hates foreign food,' explained one anxious mother, 'he's never going to eat olives wrapped in larks' tongues. Plus I hear they're

doing naked wrestling and chariot racing and that when the family go out to the forum they leave Timmy on his own at the domus with a couple of slave girls,' added the mother of the fifteen-year-old. 'He must be very bored.'

Parents hoping to hear how their children were getting on have asked why they have not received even a

single phone call, and have had it explained to them that the telephone will not be invented for another 1,700 years. A message from Timmy to his parents is expected to reach them at some point next year.

Other parents are even more concerned. One boy from a devout Christian family is rumoured to have been thrown to the lions, while another particularly rude child is believed to have been sold into slavery and was last heard of working as a galley slave in the Aegean. But the headmaster of Spencer House was unrepentant: 'Spencerians are incredibly resilient young individuals. If one of our chaps has been sold into slavery, I know he'll make a damn good go of it and come back all the stronger.'

Leaving card makes little effort to hide workmates' contempt

31 July

Business publisher Daniel Jackson left his job yesterday with a farewell card that set a new record for thinly veiled hatred from former work colleagues.

From the extra 'o' on the 'We're soo sorry you're leaving' to the unashamedly joyful sign-off 'Bye then!', the blatant sarcasm in Jackson's leaving card exposed the suppressed loathing with which he was clearly regarded.

'Who'll put the world to rights now?' wrote Jill Sanders, a long-standing colleague of Jackson, referring to his vaguely racist but freely shared standpoint on illegal immigrants. Also alluded to was Jackson's lack of support for his team members, despite maintaining that he was the most conscientious in the office. 'Congratulations on having zero lates on your record – how will we cope without your tireless efforts?'

wrote one colleague. Nor did the little smiley emoticons after supposedly ironic rudeness disguise the sincerity of the words. 'Thank God – I thought you'd never leave :)', 'joked' his long-suffering assistant.

Psychologist Emily Sole, who has made a study of office politics, says leaving cards commonly permit a venting of 'latent anger' felt against particularly disliked members of staff. 'Often, colleagues feel bound by manners to maintain a façade of politeness in the leaving card. But in extreme cases you can see the cracks beginning to appear. Look how many impersonal "Good lucks" there are. He must have been a total shit.'

Jackson, however, appeared to be completely unaware of the barely concealed contempt in his card. 'I always brought out the best in my workmates and my leaving party was exactly the same,' he boasted. 'It was quite funny actually, once they'd had a few drinks a couple of the guys started singing "Fuck off, Jackson . . . " to the tune of the Hallelujah Chorus. It's only because I have such an excellent sense of humour that they knew I'd appreciate the irony.'

50-YEAR RULE WAS ABOLISHED 50 YEARS AGO

1 August

Official government papers released under the 50-year rule bill have revealed that the 50-year rule was abolished fifty years ago, but the government couldn't tell us until now.

The announcement has caused considerable embarrassment in Whitehall, with political correspondents demanding to know how this anomaly was allowed to continue. The government, however, refused to offer any explanation, claiming that they were now protected from releasing any more information under the terms of the recent Freedom of Information Act.

This is the second embarrassment for the beleaguered Home Office in one week following the scandal surrounding the Serious Fraud Office. It turned out that they weren't the Serious Fraud Office at all, but a bunch of impostors.

Charity launches Guide Dogs for the Late

2 August

Campaigners for people with a punctuality disorder have trained the first-ever Guide Dogs for the Late.

The assistance dogs are specially trained to notice when their tardy owners start to dawdle on the way to an appointment. Their new companions then race to the appropriate destination, tugging their owners away from such time-wasting distractions as shop windows, interesting cloud formations or 'scenic routes'.

Initial trials proved very successful. Consistently late people who had been asked to attend a ten o'clock meeting all arrived at ten o'clock despite having thought they might perhaps stop off for a coffee or top up their mobile phones on the way.

This step had been promised some years ago, but the Royal Society for the Late said the delay had been unavoidable because they'd had 'some other stuff they had to do'.

RUSSIA BANS SMOKING IN OPERATING THEATRES

There was a rare victory for the Russian anti-smoking lobby yesterday after surgeons were banned from smoking while they carried out critical operations.

Moscow Surgeon Yuri Grogov was furious with what he declared to be a major infringement of his personal freedom. 'These stories of ash being dropped into open wounds are wildly exaggerated,' he insisted. 'One or two cigarette ends being left inside patients during open-heart surgery doesn't mean you should take away the pleasure of smoking for thousands of Russian surgeons.'

Teenagers to be inoculated against adolescence

The Ministry of Health launched a new scheme today that will see teenagers being inoculated against the risk of adolescence.

The jab contains a new vaccine that scientists claim will protect them from grumpiness, chronic acne, pointless petty arguments with their parents and the belief that the death of Kurt Cobain was a significant historical event.

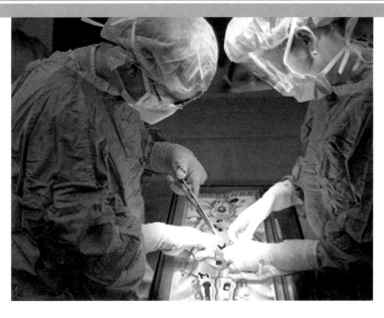

MAN DIES AFTER SURGEON TRAINED BY PLAYING OPERATION

Games manufacturer MB Games were today taken to court by a newly qualified surgeon over the accuracy of their medical game Operation.

Mr Martin Clough claims that a man lost his life on his operating table after complications following attempts to remove butterflies from his stomach. 'The game is completely inaccurate,' said Mr Clough. 'By the time we realized his nose wasn't going to light up and make a buzzing sound, he had lost too much blood.'

UNDAUNTED OLD PERSON IS DOING SOMETHING NORMALLY DONE BY YOUNG PEOPLE

4 August

At the ripe old age of eighty-one, Maud Harrison might be expected to take things a little bit easy, perhaps putting her feet up for a cup of tea after a trip to the shops to collect her pension and a tin of Whiskas for the cat.

But Maud is not one to let her age stand in the way of new experiences. Like countless get-up-and-go grannies around the country, this amazing old person is going to do something normally done by young people.

'At first I couldn't decide which pastime normally associated with young people I should take up,' said Maud, who has three great-grandchildren. 'I read about the parachuting pensioners, the marathon-running granddads and the disco-dancing grandmas and realized that there wasn't much left. And that's when I hit on the new hobby for my old age. I'm not going to let my advanced years stop me from binge drinking!'

So on Saturday night, Maud went into the town centre of her nearest provincial market town and got completely off her face on lager, cider, Bacardi Breezers and rum and blacks. 'I can keep up with all the young ones!' boasted Maud, who wears a miniskirt, crop top and strapless red bra for her drunken nights out. 'On Saturday I had six pints of snakebite, drank a load of Bacardi Breezers and then I started chucking lager bottles at the police, shouting, "Fucking bastards!" and crying hysterically because they were dragging off my mates who'd got into a fight.'

'Maud is an inspiration to us all,' said PC Willoughby, who'd been hit by a glass bottle thrown by Maud while arresting a couple of her younger binge-drinking companions. 'The energy and can-do attitude of some of Britain's elderly never cease to amaze me. I would have arrested Maud too, but I didn't want her puking in the van. Anyway, by then she was having unprotected sex in full view of everyone with a bloke she'd just met. It gives us all hope, doesn't it!'

Supermarket staff strike over anthropomorphism

9 August

The entire staff of a south London supermarket walked out last night after management placed stickers on the toilets saying, 'If you use me, please leave me clean'.

IF YOU USE ME, PLEASE LEAVE ME CLEAN

'First we had the trolley with stickers saying, "If you find me, I may be lost",' said Jack Blake, shop steward and the union's joint metaphysics officer. 'Then it was "Try me, I'm great!" on the exotic fruits. These are inanimate objects. They do not have the power of speech. The toilet label is one objective pronoun too far.'

Paisley and McGuinness brought together via miracle of Photoshop

Northern Ireland awoke to a new era of peace this morning thanks to the latest digital-imaging techniques.

Utilizing the latest Photoshop software, Tony Blair and Irish Premier Bertie Ahern toiled into the early hours, cutting and pasting images of DUP and Sinn Fein members together to create a new power-sharing assembly at Stormont.

'Gosh,' admitted a bleary-eyed Mr Blair. 'It's been a lot of hard work, but the results speak for themselves.' He added, 'Photoshop allows us to give the impression that these guys are all in the same room at the same time, and getting on like a house on fire. Of course if they were all in the room at the same time then the House probably would be on fire, and we'd all be running for cover.'

In one image DUP leader and new First Minster Dr Ian Paisley is seen grinning and doing bunny ears behind the head of Sinn Fein's Martin McGuinness. In another photo, Sinn Fein President Gerry Adams is seen gazing up adoringly at the Revd Paisley, who is also pictured leading a conga-line of nationalist and republican MPs across the floor of the House.

Mr Ahern, who got the software free with a laptop given to him at Christmas, said, 'The hardest bit was to avoid goofy stuff like putting Ian's head on a naked woman's body, and finding a half-decent picture of Martin was a nightmare. We asked McGuinness if he had ever organized his own shoot and he went a bit red. All we said was, 'We need to blow up Ian Paisley's head,' and he mumbled something about 'knowing some boys down in Fermanagh'.

Mr Brown today had nothing but praise for Adobe Photoshop, suggesting that the possibilities it offered were almost limitless. However, Adobe later issued a statement saying that any attempts to put a picture of Gordon Brown smiling beside Tony Blair might cause the software to crash, resulting in permanent damage to the computer.

ARTISTIC CLASSICS TO BE UPDATED WITH TATTOOS

12 August

Many of the most famous works of art in history are to be permanently altered in order to attract the interest of teenagers. The move will see the adding of tattoos and piercings to priceless works of art in the National Gallery, Tate Britain and other major European galleries.

'We have to reflect society's current thinking on what actually constitutes beauty,' said Culture Secretary Tessa Jowell. 'Painting tattoos on to famous paintings is simply adding embellishments that the artist would have included if they had been alive today.'

Work has already started with the Rokeby Venus by Velázquez, who now has a Harley Davidson-style wing tattoo skilfully applied to her lower back. The Venus de Milo will soon have a prominent piercing through her navel. Manet's classic 'Le déjeuner sur l'herbe' will see the central naked lady figure's arm wrapped in Maori symbolism, in deference to the influential artist Robbie Williams. In Seurat's 'Bathers at Asnières', the boy with the hat has had his forearm adorned in pointillistic style with his mother's name in Hindi.

Just like real tattoos, the alterations will be permanent. 'They'll be stuck with it for life,' said a tutting middle-aged curator. Many other works are expected to be affected, including paintings by the Pre-Raphaelites and several portraits of the Queen, who will benefit from an eyebrow stud and teardrop tattoo under her eye.

'This will re-engage thousands of teenagers who are currently unable to relate to the outmoded imagery and religious iconography in our galleries,' added the Culture Secretary. 'Now the Virgin Mary weeps because she has just run out of credit on her mobile phone.'

If the initiative proves a success, further expressions of modern beauty are likely to be added. It is understood that several Vermeer paintings will have holes punched in them so that chunky Argos jewellery and topical charity wristbands can be added, and the Mona Lisa may be livened up a bit with a ring through her nose and fingerless gloves. And the mystery of her enigmatic expression is solved at last. She's smiling because she's listening to a good track on her iPod.

Man from Hull offers to keep everyone's old audio tapes 13 August

A 58-year-old man from Hull has offered to store any unwanted cassette tapes in his home.

Music fan Alan Farrell fears that the demise of the cassette may cause many people to start throwing out their old pre-recorded and home-made compilation tapes and so he has volunteered to put as many as he can in his loft, spare room and garage.

Farrell plans to store the cassettes along with other media already in his possession, which include VHS tapes, vinyl records, old music magazines and free DVDs given away with newspapers. 'You could pay fifty pence for some of these compilation tapes at a car-boot sale,' said Farrell. 'I'll definitely get round to listening to them all at some point.'

SAINSBURY'S LAUNCHES NEW 'GULLIBLE' RANGE

14 August

Sainsbury's are doing away with the confusion of multiple labels describing products as 'organic' or 'fair-trade' and instead will be rebranding these foodstuffs as part of their new 'Gullible' range.

'Our research shows that people are prepared to pay a little bit more for products that are ethically or environmentally sound,' said a Sainsbury's spokesman. 'Now, with the Gullible range, they can see at a glance why they are having to pay that little bit more.'

A quick tour of the shelves reveals a wide choice of products. While conventional large round red tomatoes are still selling at around £2.50 a kilo, small yellow tomatoes cost around twice as much. Crisps that are flavoured with 'sea salt and cider vinegar' are also included in the Gullible range, as are bottles of olive oil with old leaves still inside.

One happy shopper spent nearly twice as much as usual by only buying products from the Gullible range. 'These organic lettuces are produced without the use of pesticides,' said mother-of-two Davina Sutton. 'You'd obviously want to pay a bit more for a lettuce with flies and slugs on it.'

As she proceeded to the checkout it was explained to Ms Sutton that all the extra profits from the new Gullible range were given over to the African farm workers who produced the goods.

'Gosh really?'

'Durr.'

She then traded in seven thousand Sainsbury's vouchers that she'd collected from her children's primary school to claim the special 'Fitness for Kids' free tennis ball.

US conservatives defend 'the right to bear fat'

15 August

A hamburger restaurant in Ohio was the scene of the latest horrific images to shock America yesterday as a strange loner dressed in a clown costume went on an indiscriminate two-hour spree giving out hamburgers, fries and chicken dippers that in twenty years' time would kill the customers from heart disease and diabetes.

'It was horrible,' said one witness. 'Everywhere you looked there was oil and mayo oozing out of the burgers, ketchup splattered over the tables, shakes spilled across the floor. How could anybody let this happen?'

The shocking scenes come as America's annual death toll from weight-related mortalities continues to mount, and many are now questioning the Republicans' treasured 'right to bear fat'. 'The current situation is insane,' said one campaigner for bun control. 'Anybody, no matter what their dietary history, is allowed to just wander into a shop and buy a burger. It's lethal. They can buy three or four burgers at a time if they want, and they often do.'

Nearby hospitals were said to be unable to admit any more obesity cases through their doors. 'The normal doors aren't wide enough. We have to use the service entrance round the back.' Thousands of very fat people die every year in the United States, where it is quite normal for people to have potato chips on their bedside table or keep a doughnut in their car.

The current laws were defended by Bob Lubbock of the National Waffle Association: 'The right to bear fat is in the US Constitution. I will stand up for this right, as soon I can get out of this chair. If a man wants a portion of ribs, or a king-size burger or fried chicken wings, or all three with mayo on top, that is his inalienable right as a US citizen. Now pass the maple syrup, would you?'

Senator Lubbock was then rushed to hospital complaining of chest pains. As he was wedged into the back of the ambulance he shouted, 'Remember nachos don't kill people. People eating nachos kill people.'

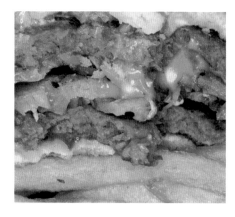

Holiday cottage shower-dial 'changed temperature gradually'

16 August

North Londoners John and Annabel Coleman rented a country cottage near Southwold in Suffolk over the weekend but were shocked to discover an unprecedented flaw in the property's plumbing system.

Taking a shower early on Saturday morning, Mr Coleman decided he would like the water to be a tiny bit warmer and so turned the dial very slightly clockwise. 'I couldn't believe it,' said Mr Coleman. 'I had been expecting the water to bubble out as if from the spout of a boiling kettle, leaving third-degree burns on my face and chest.'

Instead the shower simply increased the temperature by a few degrees. When Mr Coleman turned the dial back down again the water failed to drop to a sub-arctic freezing ice spray.

Emergency plumbers were immediately called out to rectify the situation and the cottage owners offered the couple a full refund. 'We have no idea how this happened,' said the owner. 'The property has now been fitted with a brand new, top-of-the-range shower system. Next time Mr Coleman stands under the shower, he will find that no water comes out whatsoever.'

Prince Harry to split with Tequila

17 August

Following weeks of speculation Buckingham Palace has announced that Prince Harry has split with long-time partner Tequila.

The break was said to be amicable and both sides asked that they might be allowed some privacy at this difficult time.

Over the past few years Tequila has been a constant companion of the young royal, despite claims that the glamorous Mexican brought out the worst in him. Rumours that he had slept with Tequila seem to be confirmed when they were snapped lying motionless in a gutter together. But the pressure of always being in the public eye obviously put a strain on the relationship as Harry found himself constantly being expected to walk in a straight line or just stand up.

Some observers think there may be more to the split as Harry has recently been spotted in upper-class nightclubs lovingly clutching a string of other drinks, including whisky, champagne and a member of the Guinness family. After one last night with Tequila, Prince Harry was said to be suffering from a powerful headache, dehydration and intense nausea and asked to be left alone as he swore that he and Tequila were definitely finished. But an anonymous source from Highgrove commented, 'He always says never again in the morning, but then he remembers all the good times. They'll be back together before the pubs close.'

Satanist 'denied the right to express her faith' at work

18 August

A devout Satanist working at a British Airways check-in desk has been banned from wearing items of clothing or jewellery that reveal her faith when she is dealing with members of the public.

Mrs Eileen Johnson, 43, has been a practising Satanist for many years but has come into increasing confrontation with her bosses at British Airways who claim that the wearing of devil masks, pointy horns or a blood-soaked goat's head transgressed their uniform policy and might offend customers of other faiths.

'This is religious persecution, pure and simple,' said Mrs Johnson, who worked at British Airways' Heathrow check-in desk. 'Why is it acceptable for a Muslim to wear a jihab, or a Sikh to wear a turban, while people of my religion are told it's not acceptable to wear a horned wolf-mask when dealing with customers?'

Mrs Johnson plans to take her case to an employment tribunal, claiming religious discrimination, but British Airways management were adamant that she would not be dealing with members of the public for the foreseeable future. 'While we respect the individual faiths of our staff, be they Christian, Muslim or, er, devil worshippers, we have a policy that requires all employees to observe our uniform code,' said a BA spokesman. 'It wasn't just her appearance. Mrs Johnson was communicating her Satanic beliefs with anxious passengers prior to take off. She would say, "Did you pack all the luggage yourself?" and then mumble, "You will die today and enter the kingdom of Lucifer", or "Has your luggage been left unattended at any time? Your plane will burn like the fires of hell." We had a number of complaints . . . '

Mrs Johnson said she apologized if occasionally the depth of her religious convictions affected the way she dealt with the public. 'When a Christian says "God Bless", or a Hindu presses their palms together, that apparently is all right. But you poke *one* customer with a three-pronged fork and suddenly that's unacceptable.'

WIND FARMS CLOSE AS EU IMPORTS CHEAPER WIND FROM THIRD WORLD

19 August

British wind farmers are facing bankruptcy after European Union trade rules have left them unable to compete against cheaper wind from Africa and the Far East.

'I'm facing complete ruin,' said Giles Merridon, from Cumbria. 'This wind farm has been in my family for five, maybe six years. But it's just not viable any more. A whole way of life is disappearing from our countryside.'

However, one enterprising former wind farmer has managed to survive by setting up the Powys Wind Farm Heritage Museum. 'We have guides dressed in traditional 2001 clothes. We have an interactive model of the National Grid as it was at the turn of the century. And the entire Visitor Centre is powered by traditional British wind power. Except there was no breeze again today, so we had another power cut.'

POLICE TO TACKLE BIKE CRIME WITH NEW 'INDIFFERENT SQUAD'

working, with the lid off NOW! Kev, Bob, where are those bloody duplicates? Sheena move, we need back-up pens on the other side of the counter. I want the standard letter off to the insurance company by November at the latest!"'

The theft from the bicycle turned out to be unusual in that the entire crime had been clearly recorded on CCTV and the thief had dropped his wallet in the act of removing the front wheel. Not only did it have his photo ID, address and contact details, it also contained a piece of paper entitled 'names and addresses of all the criminals who buy stolen bikes off me'.

The head of the Indifferent Squad said, 'Luckily the bike owner brought that wallet to the attention of the Indifferent Squad, otherwise we'd never have been able to pass it on to Lost Property.'

20 August

The rise in bicycle crime in the capital is to be tackled head on with the formation of an élite new police team to be known as the 'Indifferent Squad'.

The highly trained force will be stationed at key points behind the counter at London's last few remaining police stations, poised to do a bit of paperwork on stolen bicycles the moment they have dealt with everything else.

'It was amazing to see them in action,' said TV producer Pat Farrell, who is shadowing the Indifferent Squad prior to making an ITV drama on their tense and exciting work. 'At 9.03 a.m. the call came in: front wheel stolen from a Marin mountain bike on Barnes High Street. Immediately the shouting began, "Code Red! Repeat: Code Red! Dave, get form 7b/32/b from the file, don't piss about, I want a biro,

Newspapers celebrate 'prettiest ever' A Level students

Office 'nutter' did actually have serious mental-health problems

21 August

An office worker from Manchester has finally been sectioned under the Mental Health Act after desperate pleas to his workmates went ignored or were greeted with a long-suffering chuckle about what a 'complete nutter' he was.

Greg Carrick, 31, had been working at an insurance assessors for five years and regularly attempted to alert his colleagues about his concerns for his own sanity. 'Oh, yeah, Greg was always telling us how mad he was!' laughed Carrie Hooper, who worked alongside him. 'He was like the office loony, who was continually making us laugh with all the mental things he did!'

One example that a number of Greg's office colleagues cited with a nostalgic chuckle was the Christmas Party. At a time when a number of employees were consuming far too much sparkling wine, Greg went one better and downed a massive overdose of sleeping tablets and assorted tranquillizers. 'We had to rush him to hospital to get his stomach pumped – but that's Greg for you! Completely bonkers!'

On Comic Relief day Mr Carrick spent four hours standing on the window ledge of the fourteenth floor, threatening to jump. Down at street level, the police and fire brigade rushed to the scene, but when Greg's colleagues shook their collection tins and explained it was all for charity, the emergency services made a donation and were soon on their way. 'We've got a nutter like that back at the station,' chuckled one policeman. 'He'll do anything for a laugh!'

The situation reached a climax last Friday when a number of the office staff went for a drink after work and 'probably had one too many', admitted Mr Carrick's supervisor. 'And you'll never guess what Mad Greg did. He only went and set fire to a number of public buildings claiming that God had told him to do so! He's a bloody head-case, he is, he ought to be locked up!'

In fact Mr Carrick has now been locked up; he was taken into care by his local social-service department over the weekend and is now in a secure residential unit. His workmates have sent him a little placard to put up above his bench in the hospital workshop. It says, 'You don't have to be mad to work here, but it helps.'

BBC ADMITS PUDSEY 'FAKED EYE INJURY'

22 August

In the latest of the series of scandals rocking the BBC, Director-General Mark Thompson today admitted that Pudsey bear, iconic figurehead of the Children in Need appeal, had no eye problems whatsoever.

Microsoft receive first ever Error Report

24 August

There were scenes of jubilation at the headquarters of Microsoft in Redmond, Washington, yesterday, when the first Microsoft user clicked on the 'send' button after reading the Error Message.

Norman Windlesham's version of Word on Windows XP had been running trouble-free for nearly two hours when it unexpectedly froze, losing a short article about Edward II that he had been writing for an amateur history magazine.

'Just out of curiosity I clicked on the "Send Error Report" icon rather than "Don't Send" as I normally do,' said Mr Windlesham from his home in Purley. 'But I never expected to hear back from them. Imagine my excitement when I got a message back almost instantly from Bill Gates himself. I was absolutely delighted!' The message reads: 'Thank God there's someone out there! For the last ten years we thought everyone was deliberately ignoring us! Stay there – don't move!'

A crack squad of six highly trained XPerts™ was immediately dispatched, arriving at Mr Windlesham's house the following day, only to find that Mr Windlesham had turned his PC off and then on again, and the problem seemed to have gone away. 'They looked very disappointed. Especially when I said I was thinking of getting an iBook anyway.'

His apparent injury was faked in an attempt to win sympathy and extract more money from the big-hearted British general public.

In a stunned press conference at BBC TV Centre he went on to confess that Pudsey was also 'not a real bear', but just a made-up character specifically designed to appeal to impressionable young children. 'We sincerely apologize to everyone who has been misled into donating over the years in the belief that they are helping to restore sight to real one-eyed bears. We are looking into the possibility of refunding the hundreds of millions of pounds given since Pudsey first appeared in 1985.'

The damaging story comes at the end of a week of scandals that have rocked the BBC, including the revelation that Terry Wogan's hair was faked and that *Saturday Kitchen* was filmed on a Friday, and in the lounge. In an effort to win back viewers who have been put off by the damaging publicity the BBC has unveiled a competition in which callers can vote for what they think has been this week's most embarrassing scandal. Calls cost £1 and the winner will be announced whilst lines are still open.

Canal-boat chase ends in capture after eight days

An eight-day police chase across two counties ended peacefully when a suspected canal-barge thief was cornered in a canal basin near Wolverhampton.

When the emergency call came in last week, police officers ran to their specially equipped police canal barge with sirens and tracking equipment, which has been fitted out for exactly this sort of low-speed chase across the inland waterways of Britain.

The dramatic pursuit captured the nation's attention when twenty-four-hour TV news channels used helicopters to follow the brightly coloured canal boat *Esmeralda* along the length of the Worcester & Birmingham Canal. Police Inspector Harry Graham, head of the thirty-strong pursuit team, blamed an initial delay on the need to get permission from British Waterways to exceed the 4 m.p.h. speed limit. 'When we got the necessary clearance, we found our boat would only do four miles per hour anyway. So we decided on a softly-softly approach and dug in for the long haul.'

As crowds gathered on the towpath to witness the police giving cold pursuit, the leader of the canal-barge thieves seemed to be revelling in his notoriety, giving onlookers a friendly wave as he took a puff on his pipe and gave a slight nudge to the tiller to avoid a family of ducks up ahead.

But, finally, the superior training and tactics of the professionals won out when the fugitive and his wife stopped for lunch at a waterside pub and in a dramatic climax were cut off by a whole squad of police canal barges surrounding the stolen boat. Released from police custody without charge, holidaymaker Derek Aitcheson said, 'Me and the missus had no idea we'd taken the wrong barge. We wondered about the helicopters and the boat behind with the blue lights but put it down to some kind of festival.'

Looking tanned and relaxed, Inspector Graham told reporters, 'The successful end to this chase has shown that the investment in these police canal barges was money well spent.' Unfortunately the press conference had to be cut short as the shock news came in that a pedalo thief was getting away along the beach front at Paignton.

Heroin addicts demonstrate against new playground

29 August

Heroin addicts in Dundee are protesting against the loss of their traditional gathering place after the local council turned it into a children's playground.

For years the patch of barren land behind the vandalized lock-up garages had been home to heroin and crack addicts, prostitutes, pimps and drug-pushers. But the site was cleared last year and the council have now opened a colourful children's playground and one o'clock club.

'This place used to be really special. I took heroin here as a kid, and my father before me, whoever he was,' said heroin and crack addict 'Skez'.

'Me and the guys used to crap and puke here; we'd pick fights with each other and then forget what we were fighting about. It was littered with used needles, old condoms and cotton swabs, but now look at it. Red and yellow slides and swings and climbing frames with safety matting underneath. It breaks my heart to see it like this.'

Some of the addicts attempted to continue shooting up on the site but claim they were made to feel unwelcome by the newcomers. 'It's as if the council and everyone are saying, "We'd rather see children and young mums than drug addicts and prostitutes,"' said Skez, adding, 'Can you spare any change?'

A spokesman for the council commented, 'This site was cleared over a year ago, but the drug addicts have only just realized.'

Birmingham bride 'gutted' by death row rejection

31 August

LOUISE DALEY, A 32-YEAR-OLD COUNTER CLERK FOR LLOYDS TSB, HAS SUFFERED THE ULTIMATE HUMILIATION OF BEING JILTED AT THE ALTAR BY HER DEATH ROW FIANCÉ.

Louise had met her intended through a pen-friends charity, and a postal romance had blossomed. But confronted with his wife-to-be just before he was about to be executed, Freddie 'the Fridge' Rodriguez decided that he didn't love her after all and he would rather hold out for 'that special someone'.

'I just feel so stupid,' said Louise. 'I thought I had a chance for love, and it turned out just the same as with that Italian millionaire I met online last year – I'm alone, heartbroken and out of pocket to the tune of several thousand pounds. All I want is a husband. If you can't find someone willing to commit for the last few minutes before he is executed, what hope is there?'

SCHOOL ADMISSIONS ROW; NON-WIZARDS OFFERED HOGWARTS

1 September

The row over this year's secondary-school admissions took an unexpected turn today as it emerged that parents who had failed to get their child into their first choice local comprehensive were being placed by their local education authority at Hogwarts School of Witchcraft and Wizardry instead.

'I don't want my daughter flying around on a bloody broomstick,' said Karen Matthews, mother of Chelsea,

11, who has been told by her local authority that Hogwarts is the only available school in their area. 'She wants to get her GCSEs and then get a normal job. How many companies are recruiting young people who can turn their customers into cats, for Christ's sake?'

But with fewer wizard and witch children applying to Hogwarts this year, the shortfall will have to be made up by so-called 'Muggles' or non-wizards, despite fears that this may lead to bullying and division. 'We want to build inclusive and multi-faith schools,' said Education Minister Ed Balls. 'Parents should keep an open mind about considering City Academies that specialize in wizardry and magic.'

Other parents have objected to their children being offered Hogwarts on other grounds. 'The thing that really gets me about this,' said parent Duncan McEwan, 'is that the only secondary-school place they have offered my child is at a fictional school that doesn't really exist. As things stand, come September my daughter is supposed to go to King's Cross station, where she will run into a wall expecting to emerge on platform 9¾ to catch the Hogwarts Express. Whereas in fact she will simply run into a wall and probably bruise herself quite badly.'

The government said it would look into claims that other Year 6 students have been offered places at fictional schools such as St Trinian's, Bash Street School and Grange Hill, but insisted that the school for wizardry made famous by J. K. Rowling did exist. 'Hogwarts is every bit as real as the government's policy of parental choice.'

Teenage 'joyriders' stealing pensioners' electric scooters

2 September

Underage criminals in the Isle of Wight are stealing pensioners' electric scooters and using them to race one another or attempt dangerous high-speed stunts.

Residents on Shanklin's notorious Eastcliffe estate cannot sleep for the noise from the scooters' whirring electric motors and the youngsters' screaming as the so-called 'joyriders' attempt to perform handbrake turns, wheelies and 360-degree spins. 'These things only go about eight miles an hour, so they are completely wasting their time,' said Inspector Ray Charteris of the island's traffic police. 'They steal them in an attempt to go joyriding, but it's more a case of "misery-riding" really.'

NUDE PROTEST ORGANIZED BY CREEPY MAN WITH NO INTEREST IN CLIMATE CHANGE

3 September

Hundreds of climate-change protesters this week answered a call from a previously unknown organization calling itself 'Naked Action for Global Warming', following an initiative from a middle-aged man from the West Midlands with an interest in amateur photography.

Bryan Davidson put out a call on various environmental websites calling on all concerned protesters to strip off to draw attention to the destruction of the ozone layer. Since he was unable to travel to an alpine glacier or the North Pole he proposed that the mass nude protest take place 'in the woods near my house'. A large number of students,

green campaigners and eco-warriors arrived at Mr Davidson's Redditch home for the photo opportunity and were each vetted for suitability by the lone organizer.

'He said I was perfect,' said Olga Schmidt, 24, from the Czech Republic. 'But my grandmother who had travelled with me wasn't quite right for the message of "concerned youth" that he was eager to communicate. He photographed us in the nude pointing up to the sky, and then crouching to search for dying insects, and then he filmed me jumping up and down to show I was "hopping mad" about the vanishing ice sheets.' Mr Davidson ended the photo-shoot by getting all the naked protesters to hug and kiss one another 'to show the love that could defeat climate change'.

Subsequent research has shown that Mr Davidson has no history of environmental campaigning, although his name did crop up as having been blacklisted from a number of swinging parties after promising that 'his wife would be coming along later'. But the protesters were quick to defend Mr Davidson. 'No, he was very concerned about global warming, explaining that we must still rub sun cream all over our bodies even though it was cloudy,' said Olga. 'He even offered to do me himself.'

NEW REALITY TV SHOW WILL PUT MARTYRS IN 'PARADISE'

5 September

A new reality TV show plans to trick Muslim extremists into thinking they are taking part in a suicide bombing, and then secretly filming them as they explore what they imagine is the afterlife.

Following the success of the TV show *Space Cadets*, in which contestants were duped into believing that they had been sent into orbit, Channel 4 has been under pressure to raise the stakes in the competitive world of reality TV. 'If death is the ultimate reality, then making the participants think they are dead is the ultimate reality TV show,' said producer Jeremy Gill. 'These young extremists will really think they have died for the jihad and gone to their Islamic paradise.'

The show's set-up is quite simple. Militant young Muslims will be tricked into thinking that they are about to lay down their lives in the holy jihad. But instead, the suicide bombs in their suitcases will only be stun grenades. When they wake up they will have no idea that they are actually in a specially prepared aircraft hangar outside Luton.

'They believe that seventy-two virgins will be waiting for them in paradise. In our version, there is only Christine Hamilton and Carol Thatcher,' explained the producer of *Jihad Martyrs*. 'We thought it would be more entertaining if paradise was consistently disappointing and very badly run. Nothing works and the food is awful. Oh and God and St Peter will there too, because these guys have to adjust to waking up in a Judaeo-Christian heaven. And we made God Jewish. Channel 4 does have a remit to cater for all faiths, and we wouldn't want to cause any offence.'

The programme is already in production and the first episode will transmit next month. Police will not be informed of the identity of the suicide bombers until the end of the series, nor the secret location in which the programme is being filmed. 'We thought it might compromise the illusion that these people were in heaven,' said Jeremy Gill, 'if armed policemen suddenly burst in and pumped thirty bullets into their heads.'

Whale gives birth listening to CD of humans shouting at each other

6 September

Marine biologists completing a six-year study into the ideal conditions for whale birthing have discovered that the most positive response from whales in labour came from those listening to CDs of human beings shouting at one another.

'It should have occurred to us earlier,' said Professor Damien Fielden. 'We'd tried the sound of gently lapping waves, birdsong and Beethoven's "Pastoral" Symphony and none of it was helping the mother whale in the slightest.'

It was then that one of the researchers accidentally left on the underwater audio equipment while an argument developed on the project's floating laboratory. 'We'd all been cooped up on this boat for so long and suddenly it all poured out – how much we all hated one another, how "Miser" Mike had bad breath and Dave was a smug academic snob. We didn't realize that the microphone was still live and that the whales were hearing every word of it.'

But birthing whales began swimming from miles around to listen to the sounds of human shrieking, and further studies revealed that angry shouting actively helped the whales achieve the calm inner peace that they seek when bringing a baby whale into the world.

The scientists then sent out a team to record the most heated human arguments that they could find: a man trying to pay his gas bill over the telephone, the queue for the returns desk at IKEA, Alex Ferguson talking to the fourth official, the Northern Ireland assembly, and a Democratic feminist debating abortion with a Republican creationist.

'All that anger and swearing really seemed to help the whales. It makes up for all those years of failed experiments with "land births". Finally we had created the perfect birthing environment for these gentle and sensitive creatures. One intelligent mammal helping another; it was a beautiful and spiritual moment,' said Marie-Anne Coulson. 'It was a shame that the Japanese "research scientists" then came along and harpooned them all, but you can't have everything.'

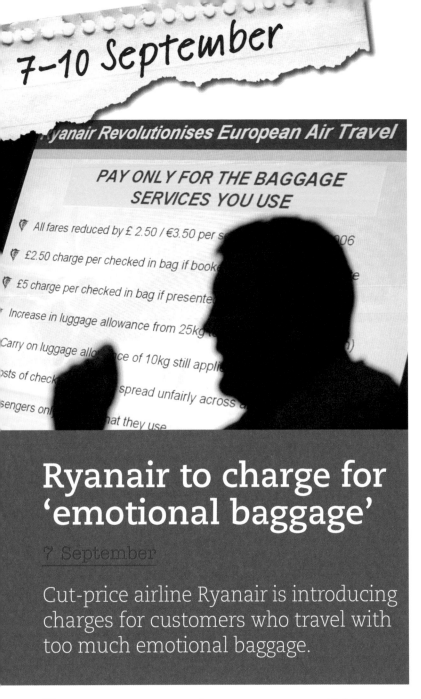

Ryanair Revolutionises European Air Travel

PAY ONLY FOR THE BAGGAGE SERVICES YOU USE

- All fares reduced by £2.50 / €3.50 per s...
- £2.50 charge per checked in bag if booke...
- £5 charge per checked in bag if presente...
- Increase in luggage allowance from 25kg ...
- Carry on luggage allo...ce of 10kg still appli...
- ...sts of check...
- ...engers onl... spread unfairly across ...
- ...at they use

Ryanair to charge for 'emotional baggage'

7 September

Cut-price airline Ryanair is introducing charges for customers who travel with too much emotional baggage.

The announcement was made in an attempt to avoid delays caused by family arguments at check-in and boarding; henceforth Ryanair will have a strict rule of 'one simple divorce case per passenger'.

One regular flyer turned up at Stansted yesterday with her grown-up son from her first marriage, who was still not talking to her second husband. 'The check-in lady asked me a series of questions about the divorce and all the suppressed anger and guilt felt by the kids, and I had to pay an extra £39.99 plus VAT,' said Sarah Johnstone. 'I complained that this sort of money-grabbing reminded me of my absent dad who just took, took, took but left me nothing in his will – and they added another £29.99.'

The new charge is part of a raft of revised tariffs from the no-frills airline, including extra payments for seats for those who opt not to stand for the duration of their flight. There has been criticism of the airline for their decision to charge for oxygen in the event of emergency. 'The oxygen masks will still drop down from the overhead lockers as required by law,' explained Michael O'Leary, 'but now the supply of oxygen is activated by a simple slot-meter that takes euros and pound coins.'

PUBLIC STAR IN FILM CLASSICS AS PUBS INTRODUCE 'MOVIE-OKE'

8 September

Pubs are fighting back against falling profits with a new craze in which members of the public get to appear in classic films alongside the stars. So-called 'Movie-oke' is the latest technological innovation from Japan and allows the player to appear in famous cinema roles, saying the lines in place of the original actor.

'It's been great for business,' said Mike Thomsett, landlord of the Market Tavern in Middlesbrough. 'The lasses have been queuing up to be Marilyn Monroe in *Some Like It Hot*. The scene on the beach where she meets Tony Curtis has been different every time. Though I don't remember Marilyn saying the line "Yer can shag us if yer buys us a kebab." Mind you, that was the same girl what threw up her breakfast in Tiffany's.'

The craze has been popular with men too, who have tended to opt for more heroic roles. Unemployed lorry driver Ron Naylor tried his hand at playing Humphrey Bogart in *Casablanca*. 'Of all the gin joints in all the towns in all the world, she walks into mine . . .' he said, adding, 'Oi, Major Strasser, are you looking at my bird? Cos you spilt my pint and I'm going to smash your face in.'

The craze is equally popular down south, where one pub reported participants joining in the famous chariot race in *Ben Hur* but tutting at everyone who didn't slow down for horses. 'The ending of *Spartacus* was a little disappointing,' said one Surrey landlord. 'One bloke shouts "I'm Spartacus", and then everyone else kept their heads down, mumbling, "Well, you're on your own then, mate – it's nothing to do with me." '

'PEOPLE PRE-JUDGE ME BECAUSE I LOOK LIKE HITLER'

10 September

Hitler look-a-like Kevin Eades says he has had enough of people thinking he is some sort of right-wing control freak because of his striking similarity to the famous Nazi dictator.

'I just happen to have the same facial structure and a similar haircut,' said Kevin, librarian and keen amateur historian. 'But people see me and immediately apply all sorts of negative associations based simply on my unfortunate appearance.'

Kevin, 57, from north London, insists that he has no particular interest in right-wing politics, although admitted that his choice of clothes and haircut do not help people separate his appearance from the man who was responsible for the death of fifty million people. 'Sure, I have a moustache, but why should I shave it off just because a few people have a problem with some long-dead foreign leader? And I like to wear smart clothes; who doesn't? That's my right in a free country and yet it seems even today there are some people determined to take these freedoms away. If it wasn't for all the Jews and Communists trying to take over the banks we wouldn't have these problems.'

Kevin says his regrettable resemblance to the greatest monster of the twentieth century has led to problems at work, where he has been suspended from dealing with members of the public at Stamford Hill Library. 'Apparently my physical appearance does not fit in with the "politically correct" template required by a minority of browsers at the library. We get a lot of Hasidic Jews in the library and one or two single-issue fanatics thought they had a right to tell the council how their librarians should dress.'

Chief librarian Brian Philpot said, 'It wasn't just the clothes. It was the way Kevin stamped the library books

with his own special Third Reich stamp. Sometimes people would be browsing in the travel section and he would demand to see their papers.'

Kevin was eventually put in the back office where he was made responsible for ordering books, but even this led to problems at the library in the predominantly Jewish part of north London. 'Can you believe the library didn't have one copy of *Mein Kampf*?' said Kevin in an increasingly noticeable German accent. 'I mean, if people could only put the politics to one side, it's a damn good read. But in my experience the Jews see anti-Semitism in everything. Hitler, Goering, Goebbels: they can't have all been anti-Semitic. So how come it's OK to be prejudiced against the Nazis, but not against gypsies and genetically defective social deviants?'

Eventually the political and personal differences between Kevin and his boss Brian led to a physical clash that saw violence between the two men breaking out in the non-fiction section of the library shelves. Kevin shoved Brian back all the way to the newspapers and magazines until Brian rallied and forced Kevin right out of the library, although the devastation wreaked will take decades to put right. 'It was a glorious victory for the People's Soviet of Stamford Hill Library,' said Stalin look-a-like Brian Philpot. 'But now the kulaks are not returning their books on time and these class enemies of the revolution must be destroyed.'

Grim Reaper realizes he was meant to collect Keith Richards 'ages ago'

12 September

A clerical error by Death, the Grim Reaper, has permitted the Rolling Stones' guitarist Keith Richards to enjoy three decades of life beyond his allotted time on Earth.

'We just found his collection form down the back of the old desk,' admitted an embarrassed Grim Reaper. 'He was due to be collected back in 1977, at the nadir of a downward spiral of heroin addiction and cocaine use.' Yet despite the raddled, deathly appearance of the ageing rock star, no one seemed to notice the bureaucratic oversight, and Richards was permitted to carry on living for thirty years longer than he was supposed to.

'It's all very embarrassing . . .' said a spokesman for the office of the Grim Reaper. 'We have apologized to Keith Richards and his family, and said that we will do our best to rectify the situation at the earliest convenient date. Although, at the time of speaking, they still haven't got back to us.'

This is not the first time that the Grim Reaper's office has let a collection slip through the net. Other major figures well past their due death-dates include Jimmy Carter, Gary Glitter and the IRA informer who was working for the British secret services.

CASHPOINTS NOW ASKING IF YOU CAN REALLY AFFORD IT

15 September

Customers of the leading high street banks have reported that automated telling machines are becoming increasingly stingy and obstructive.

Since the credit crunch started to bite earlier in the year, a number of cashpoints have started to give vague excuses about not having the right change on them, displaying messages suggesting that you might be asking for too much, or just showing half an inch of the notes requested, but then refusing to actually let go of the cash.

One frustrated HSBC customer, Luke Defrayne, recalls: 'We had a right old tug-of-war; I pulled the notes a little way out, then the machine pulled them back in again. In the end I only managed to walk away with the torn-off corner of a ten-pound note – what use is that on a Saturday night?' Mr Defrayne had wanted to withdraw a hundred pounds, as he does on a regular basis, and everything seemed normal when the machine said, 'Please take your card and wait for your cash.' 'So I waited and waited and then eventually a new message appeared, saying, "Actually, are you sure you can afford this?"'

One NatWest customer from Warrington got the twenty-seventh question wrong and was therefore refused his money. 'I know the cashpoints have to go through a few questions,' said Gordon Trowler, 'but asking me the capital of Moldova seems overly cautious. I can't believe I chose Yerevan over Kishinev, but I'd already used up my 50-50 and phoned a friend.' Other machines have been reported to display messages such as 'I'll let you have it when I've been paid', 'Why don't we take it off that money you owe for the curry?' and 'You're not having your pocket money till you've done some revision.'

'The money supply is clearly under pressure at the moment owing to the global credit crunch,' said a City insider. 'The responsibility for the global financial crisis lies with a handful of top banking executives who allowed these bad debts to build up, and the thing is, now we need all that cash to pay them their bonuses.'

MAIL TO GIVE AWAY 'BIG ISSUE LITE' TO UNDERCUT HOMELESS

17 September

Associated Newspapers are to start printing a rival magazine to give away for free wherever homeless people are trying to sell the *Big Issue*.

The new publication will be the latest in a number of free newspapers handed out at railway stations and bus terminals across Britain's major cities which have made a major dent in the sales of established newspapers over recent years. The only vendors who to date have not had to go head to head with the free sheets have been homeless people trying to make a few extra pence by selling the magazine produced especially to help them get back into mainstream society. This is now set to change with the production of the *Little Issue*, a cheaply produced free listings magazine which will contain celebrity gossip alongside shocking exposés of how the London homeless actually have large second homes in the Home Counties.

'All credit to the tramps for identifying a gap in the market,' said Paul Dacre of Associated Newspapers, which already produces *Metro* and *London Lite*. 'But we think we could exploit this sector more fully by giving our magazine away. Our vendors won't actually be homeless, although we might give them a mongrel on a bit of string or something.'

The pilot issue contained articles claiming that most of Britain's homeless were making thousands of pounds a week as part of a criminal network organized by a Serbian gangmaster, but also included homeless lifestyle features such as 'A Cardboard Box of My Own' and a wine section featuring a review of B&Q's own brand of methylated spirit. The finance section explains that the best place to beg is sitting next to a cashpoint machine, because people find it really embarrassing that they have so much cash.

'But essentially this magazine is produced by people with comfortable homes, for people who live in comfortable homes, in order to make themselves feel smug that they are not sleeping out on the streets. And frankly we're pretty confident that we are going to blow that tatty charity rag right out of the water.'

The first *Little Issue* also includes a free A3 wall chart of all the other free sheets littering Britain's big cities. 'It's not just for sticking on your wall,' said Paul Dacre. 'It also folds out into a flimsy blanket for when the homeless haven't raised enough to spend the night in a hostel.'

'With hindsight, West Indies versus Sri Lanka in the Twenty20 World Cup did not constitute a "Mega-Monday-Night Feast of Cricket", even if it was coupled in a back-to-back double-header with New Zealand versus Kenya.' Sky also apologized for telling viewers that the championship fixture between Barnsley and Preston was a 'must-see' game, that the NFL match between Denver Broncos and Miami Dolphins was part of a 'Triple-Whammy Tuesday' and that any speedway event was ever worth watching.

They also confessed that 'Survival Sunday' was not an accurate description of a day that decided which team would go down from the Blue Square Conference North to the Unibond League. 'All in all,' said the host, 'you can only watch so much sport and *Mad Men* is just starting over on BBC4 and that's really good, actually.'

Sky Sports admits forthcoming match is 'missable'

19 September

In a radical departure from its policy of advertising sporting events as 'Super Saturday' or 'Grand-Slam Sunday', the Sky Sports channel has shocked its viewers by trailing a forth-coming live sports broadcast as 'A Take-It-or-Leave-It Fixture, Purely of Academic Interest to Supporters of the Two Teams Involved'.

A spokesman said, 'It's only Leeds Rhinos versus the Warrington Something-or-Others, and, let's face it, most people don't even like Rugby League, so to bill it as "Showdown Saturday" or "Clash of the Titans" would be overselling it a bit.'

The spokesman admitted that it was not the first time the broadcaster had misled viewers.

Singapore introduces death penalty for use of irony

21 September

The Singapore government has announced plans to impose the death penalty on anyone caught using a sense of irony within its hallowed borders. Prime Minister Lee Hsien Loong delivered a patriotic speech on national television in which the new measures were announced. One watching journalist commented, 'Oh, that's really going to work, that is,' and was immediately led away by police.

105

Existence of 'horses' finally proved to be a myth

23 September

New evidence, published today, has finally proved beyond doubt that the legendary animal known by storytellers down the centuries as a 'horse' does not really exist.

The study, carried out at the University of Graham, looked into over fifty unexplained sightings of the mythical beasts over a period of six months. In one instance, academics led by Dr Jake Reilly spent over twenty minutes in the south-eastern corner of a Cumbrian field that had been the subject of a number of unsubstantiated 'horse' sightings. Not a single horse was seen. Claims that the horses had simply moved to another part of the field have been ridiculed by the doctor. He also dismissed the animals seen cantering majestically through the mist in the far corner of the field as being 'probably cows, ghosts, or maybe leopards'.

The claims have been met with anger and disbelief by members of the equestrian community. Sandra Hatton of Redruth claims to have owned horses for over forty years, saying, 'I have fed, watered and ridden horses every day for as long as I can remember. I think I would notice if they didn't exist.' Other people previously claiming to be 'horse' owners have been more circumspect.

Upon hearing the scientific proof, Mr Colin Lehman, a horse enthusiast from Cardiff, inspected his prize-winning 'steeds', only to be forced to admit that they must just be big dogs with unusually long noses and a taste for grass and sugar lumps. He told this reporter that, although he felt cheated by the dealer who sold him these horse-dogs, the animals had become part of his family, though he would stop riding them and try to train them to fetch sticks instead.

Horses have remained at the forefront of popular culture in recent years, a rise that is attributed by many to the runaway success of fantasy films such as *Black Beauty*, *The Horse Whisperer* and *Peter the Horse that Runs Around*. However, scientists believe that because many people are increasingly unable to differentiate between make-believe and real life, horses became widely accepted as being real animals. Speaking at an emotionally charged press conference, Dr Reilly said, 'I understand that these findings will cause distress and anger among many people who believe they have seen horses, or claim, in good faith, to have owned, bet on and stroked what they thought were horses. However, I stand by the conclusions of this scientific study. If anyone can provide me with irrefutable proof of the existence of horses then I will eat my own face.'

The case has clear parallels with a spate of fraudulent pet sales in 2003. Following the success of the *Lord of the Rings* trilogy there were over thirty reported cases of people having been sold strategically shaven monkeys, believing that they were hobbits. Hobbits are in fact now extinct in the wild and can only be kept in captivity under strict licensing rules.

FRENCH VERSION OF *THE APPRENTICE* NOT ALLOWED TO FIRE CONTESTANTS

A French version of the popular British reality show *The Apprentice* has come unstuck as it emerged that the host was not legally permitted to fire any of the contestants. The finalists are now insisting that they have a job for life, after an attempt to sack one competitor resulted in massive student demonstrations, major strikes across the French public sector and the burning of lorries on the autoroute.

The show has now been renamed *Restez en Place!* and follows the various contestants as they negotiate down their thirty-five-hour week and threaten to work to rule over the inadequacy of a two-hour lunch-break. Meanwhile the host, Alain de Sucre, observes their attempts in the various tasks he set them, such as selling overpriced stale baguettes at a French market in Hertfordshire or working as a Parisian waiter without smiling. After they have failed miserably he tells them what he thinks of them: 'Vous êtes une pièce de merde' or 'Vous n'avez pas un clue saignant!' before pausing for effect and delivering the show's punch-line: 'Mais . . . restez en place!'

The head of TF1 is under intense criticism for buying the rights to *The Apprentice* without checking if the BBC format could work under French employment law. 'He is totally incompetent and is not fit to run a television channel,' said one colleague. 'Mark my words – he will certainly be out of a job when he retires on full salary in 2028.'

'Last year's fashions are fine' agree London Fashion Week

Designers, stylists and models at this year's London Fashion Week have agreed to showcase the same clothes as last year since there is no point in buying a whole load of new outfits just for the sake of it.

Steve Raffell of the London Fashion Council explained: 'We looked at the dresses and everything from London Fashion Week twelve months ago, and thought, "Actually, what's wrong with all this stuff? It still fits, it's not worn out yet, it was quite expensive, so why change it?"'

There were gasps as the models stepped out on to the catwalk, showcasing outfits that had been in their wardrobe for a whole year. 'Frankly it's come as a big relief,' confessed Raffell. 'After a year racking our brains for the big new look of the season, we finally hit upon the answer to the eternal question "What is the new Black?" Well, it's black.'

Teenager remains interested in caged pet

27 September

A sixteen-year-old girl from Hendon in north London has stunned observers by remaining attentive and affectionate towards the pet rabbit that she promised to love for ever back when she was eleven.

Five years on, and despite moving on to secondary school, passing through adolescence and becoming interested in boys, music and shopping, Jennifer Timpson has broken with teenage convention by failing to abandon the pet to a life of stinking squalor in a rarely visited hutch at the bottom of the garden. 'We are very worried about her,' said her mother. 'All her brothers and sisters had pets and became progressively less attentive to them as they reached puberty. Danny's pet rat didn't even have any water towards the end, it just did the best it could sucking the moisture from the urine-soaked sawdust. Sally's hamster had been dead for a month before she even noticed. But with Jennifer it's like there's some key part of her brain that's not working, that has kept her caring for this rabbit, cleaning it out, giving it fresh vegetables and letting it out for regular periods of exercise.'

Jennifer said that she had promised she would always look after the rabbit and just because she had been a primary-school pupil when she gave her word, that didn't mean she should behave any differently now.

'She is planning to go and live in the rainforests to protect endangered species or something when she grows up,' said her distraught parents. 'Like how much money is there in that?'

'It doesn't matter, though, because her brothers and sisters will still be here to look after us in our old age,' added Mrs Timpson. 'The others are all really good children. They have promised that they will take great care of us when we are old and infirm – and definitely won't leave us abandoned in a dingy flat with no food or care for weeks on end.'

GOVERNOR OF BANK OF ZIMBABWE FORCED TO EXPLAIN INFLATION OF 1,000,003 PER CENT

29 September

Gideon Gono, the embattled governor of the Bank of Zimbabwe, has been forced to write to the President of Zimbabwe explaining why the country's inflation target of one million per cent has not been met this financial quarter.

The Zimbabwean retail price index just edged over the official target to 1,000,003 per cent, although it is hard to gain a precise guide to current prices as there is nothing in any of the shops. Official figures claim, however, that cornmeal and maize have remained steady at twenty-five million Zimbabwean dollars a kilo, though machetes and ankle irons have edged up in price owing to increased demand over the holiday period.

The governor's letter seems keen to stress that the fault of the inflation rise lies with everybody except President Mugabe, war veterans and Zanu (PF). 'Your Excellency the democratically elected President Mugabe,' he writes. 'Western imperialists and bad magic of MDC have conspiring push up inflation in our great motherland. Much bad spirits and ancestors of Morgan Tsvangirai have been spread by the one remaining white farmer who fails recognize your unanimous victory in peaceful election. Land reforms not pursued vigorous enough – all fault of mind-poison by Tony Blair, George Bush and BBC World Service.'

The last governor of the Bank of Zimbabwe also failed to meet his inflation target and disappeared soon after during an official visit to the Limpopo Crocodile Petting Zoo. But Mr Gono is keen to distance himself from the policies of his predecessor, stressing that he was not an enthusiastic-enough supporter of Mr Mugabe's genius for financial affairs.

'Only with father of nation President Mugabe will inflation follow your strict orders to drop below million per cent. Army must execute all farm animals costing too many dollars, fuel and crops must be burnt to chase out MDC evil magic – this wise Zanu (PF) policy guarantee economic stability. Aids created by imperialist US scientists drive up prices – reporters from BBC2's *Newsnight* must be forbidden broadcast sex virus with their bad sorcery. Long live President Mugabe! Vote Zanu (PF)! Must dash now, war veterans just arrived to congratulate me on my unwavering support.'

Government recognize Cod War syndrome

30 September

AFTER DECADES OF CAMPAIGNING FROM THE FORMER COMBATANTS IN THE FISHERIES DISPUTE WITH ICELAND, THE GOVERNMENT HAS FINALLY RECOGNIZED THE EXISTENCE OF COD WAR SYNDROME, AND WILL PAY COMPENSATION TO THOSE SUFFERING FROM THE CONDITION.

For years neither the Ministry of Defence nor the Department of Fisheries and Food were willing to accept responsibility for the apathy, depression and vague fishy smell that surrounded those British trawler men who had been involved in the 1970s fishing crisis. But medical opinion continued to harden about the symptoms having a direct connection to involvement in the brief stand-off over fishing quotas.

'We are the forgotten warriors,' said former fisherman Mike McLeish from Grimsby. 'Sure, the Battle of Britain pilots are all heroes, and the Falklands veterans have their medals and memorials. But when it comes to the Cod War, people imply it wasn't so important or dangerous. It's almost as if they are saying it wasn't a proper war.'

Muslim veils to feature wearer's picture

2 October

An historic compromise has been reached to allow Muslim women to continue to wear the *niqab* or full veil while still showing their face.

Under plans formed after emergency discussions between the Prime Minister and the Muslim Council of Great Britain, Islamic women can still opt to keep everything but their eyes covered, but a photo of their face will be printed on to the veil.

'Let's be under no illusions. This is an historic breakthrough,' said the Home Secretary. 'I really think we have found a Third Way on veils. Islamic law will continue to be respected, but now everyone can see whom they are talking to.'

Production of the picture veils has already started, and Islamic women are enquiring if the photos have to be recent, or if they can use more flattering pictures from fifteen years ago. The image printed on the *niqab* will also give the wearer the opportunity to convey what sort of a mood they are in on any given day. 'Muslim women will be able to buy themselves a variety of veils, one with a smile on the front for when they are feeling happy, or perhaps one with a more pensive expression for reading the Koran,' said the Home Secretary. 'But then say they were going to a funeral, they might want to choose a veil with the big sad face on it,' he added helpfully.

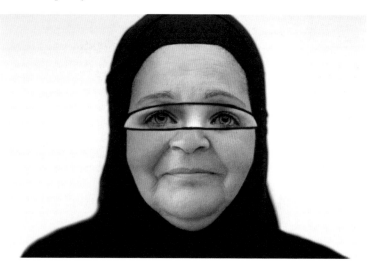

Useless middle-class soccer kids consoled with promise of nicer lives

5 October

After a severe thrashing from yet another tough-looking school, the bruised and demoralized middle-class boys from St Jude's Primary felt like giving up football altogether.

The team of eleven-year-olds had just lost 12–0, with several of the boys coming off in tears because their opponents had 'barged past them', 'been too rough' and 'had kicked the ball hard on purpose'.

But at the end of full time, Jack Randle, the team's coach and father of hapless goalkeeper Timmy, gave the miserable squad an uplifting team talk that compared the future life prospects of the soccer losers from St Jude's with the skilful and physically braver working-class boys in the other team.

'You may have lost twelve-nil today against this big bunch of bullies, but let's get things in perspective. You're going to have much nicer lives than them. They're going to be poor. You are all going to get well paid jobs in a warm dry office. They are going to have to lift heavy things in the rain for a pittance. One day, some of those eleven-year-old thugs laughing over there may develop poverty-related diseases or become drug addicts from their time in prison. Who are the losers, boys: them or you?'

At this point one or two of the other parents attempted to step in to end the talk, saying: 'Er, anyway, well tried, lads, it's just a game, eh?' but Mr Randle would not be stopped. 'Take a good look at their faces, boys. One day, one of them will be driving the minicab that takes you to the airport. You make sure you keep them waiting outside your nice big house for ages. If they are sweeping the streets in your road, drop a crisp packet as you walk past them. They have won one game of football. You are going to win the game of life.'

At this point the victorious team coach strolled across to shake hands and asked, 'Oi, didn't my team play your lot when we were kids, mate?'

Mr Randle replied, 'Definitely not. I drive a Saab Turbo, you know.'

LOVERS' GUIDE 27 FEATURES MARRIED COUPLE READING

7 October

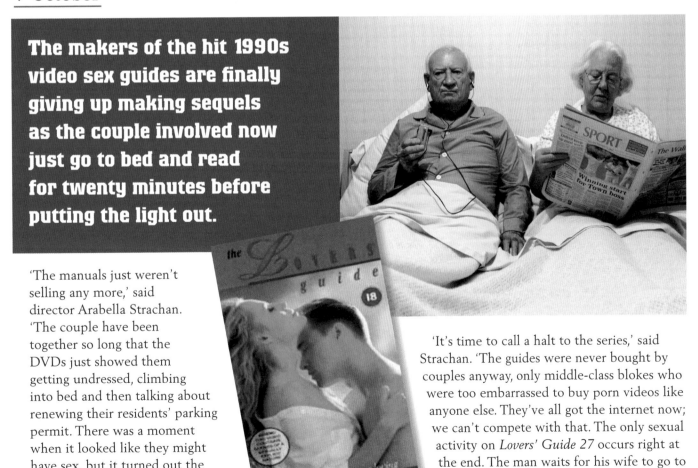

The makers of the hit 1990s video sex guides are finally giving up making sequels as the couple involved now just go to bed and read for twenty minutes before putting the light out.

'The manuals just weren't selling any more,' said director Arabella Strachan. 'The couple have been together so long that the DVDs just showed them getting undressed, climbing into bed and then talking about renewing their residents' parking permit. There was a moment when it looked like they might have sex, but it turned out the woman was just reaching across to have a sip of his Ovaltine.'

'It's time to call a halt to the series,' said Strachan. 'The guides were never bought by couples anyway, only middle-class blokes who were too embarrassed to buy porn videos like anyone else. They've all got the internet now; we can't compete with that. The only sexual activity on *Lovers' Guide 27* occurs right at the end. The man waits for his wife to go to sleep, slips downstairs on his own and then watches *Lovers' Guide 1*.'

EU RULE THAT GERMANY MUST HAVE SHORTER NOUNS

11 October

The European Commission on Languages has passed a landmark resolution against the lengths of German nouns.

The newly announced Noun Directive, or 'Der neue Deutsche Shortennounendirectivbrusselsbullscheisser ist heraus gekommen', as it was billed in the German press this morning, was first proposed back in 1998, or 'Neunzehnhundertachtundneunzig' as it is known in Germany.

Delegates from smaller European countries had reported feeling intimidated by the size of these big German words and finally Luxembourg and Denmark jointly proposed that Germany scale down its nouns to less menacing levels. Germany responded by explaining that compound nouns were part of their 'historischesprachentradition' at which point several delegates ran out of the chamber claiming 'linguistic bullying'.

British public rush to give cash to private -school 'charities'

15 October

High street collections from Britain's top public schools have raised millions of pounds over the weekend, ending any doubt as to whether élitist institutions such as Eton and Harrow deserve their charitable status.

Ordinary shoppers, spotting the collection tins being shaken on behalf of the private schools, went straight past volunteers collecting for 'less deserving charities' like Age Concern and Oxfam and rushed to stuff five-pound notes in the tins of the young toffs in top hats and tails.

'I only give to certain charities,' said Tina Cruddock, 32, mother of three, who lives on a council estate in Dudley. 'But when I heard the master of one of them posh schools talking about what marvellous charity work they do for kids whose parents can only afford twenty grand a year, well, we rushed down here to give 'em all our spare pennies.'

SPORTS FAN'S NOVELTY WIG MARKS HIM OUT AS 'A BIT OF A CHARACTER'

16 October

Sports fan Roland Harris, 36, was complimented on his adventurous sense of humour this week after a TV commentator noticed him wearing a brightly coloured, curly wig in the middle of the crowd.

Harris, 36 and from Bath, bought the luminous yellow wig at a joke shop last week after searching for an item that would reflect his unique personality and unconventional sense of humour. He was reported to be absolutely delighted with the chuckles that greeted the vision of this madcap spectator breaking all conventions at the Lord's Test between England and South Africa.

'You see, men's hair is usually quite short and either black or brown or blonde,' explained Mr Harris. 'So wearing a wig made out of long, bright yellow hair is just plain daft! My friends can't believe I'm bonkers enough to wear it out in public! But that's just the way I am!'

Mr Harris came to national attention when a TV cameraman picked him out of the crowd, and the commentator said that the wearer of the wig clearly must be 'a bit of a character'. Mr Harris went on to reveal that when live pictures of him wearing the wig were beamed around the world, several of his friends were incredulous. 'They texted me saying "ive jst seen u on tv. ur mental!!!!" and "u nutta! u shld b locked up!!!!!!", but I don't care. It's different, and it makes me look daring and interesting.' Nevertheless, some have criticized his decision for wearing such an elaborate headpiece. 'I don't think that kind of ridiculous hair should be allowed in public places,' said London mayor Boris Johnson.

Lovestalk

post your brief encounters and creepy obsessions with complete strangers . . .

• The Metropolitan Line, last Thursday evening: You were the stunning lady in the short flowery skirt who got off at Watford and then cut across the park, down past the paddling pool and that miniature railway, then over the bridge by the canal next to the woods. I lost which way you went after that. Fancy a hiking trip for two in the Lake District next weekend?

• Beckie!!! We danced into the early hours of Sunday morning last weekend at the Funky Chic club in Soho. You wrote your number on my arm but, annoyingly, I lost it on the way home. Do you think you could learn to love an amputee?

• Boulevard club in Soho last Friday night. You were the unspeakably handsome businessman in the Armani suit. I was the lap-dancer whose breasts your rugged face was nestled in. I wish I'd had the confidence to ask you for your number. Fancy a trip to the opera?

• You were the lovely girl with Tourette's, sun-bathing in Hyde Park yesterday lunchtime. I was the 'pervy bastard' you kept telling to 'piss off'. It's OK, I've read up on your condition and I know I could learn to live with it. I'd love to see more of you. TONY

• You were the sexy sales assistant at Boots in Charing Cross who sold me the ten-pack of Durex the night before last. I was the guy who was really embarrassed cos you were so beautiful. Anyway, I've still got a couple left if you fancy meeting up for a drink.

• To the pretty blonde lady sitting opposite me on the Piccadilly Line last Monday morning at about 10.30. I was the suicide bomber preparing to give up his life for the holy jihad. There was something about the way you smiled at me that made me want to carry on living. Fancy a coffee? Ah, sod it, how about a beer?

Man with 'identikit-style' face arrested again

18 October

A man from north London was arrested for the six-teenth time in three weeks last night, owing to his uncanny resemblance to the CGI face on all police 'wanted' posters.

The man, as yet unnamed, was arrested in Camden at around 3 p.m. yesterday, and then again at 7.30 p.m., once on suspicion of burglary, subsequently for an alleged mugging offence. The suspect's lawyer Mr Chris Walton said, 'The police have to pay the price for such flimsily constructed computer graphics. Every time you hear of a crime on the news it flashes up a photofit of the suspect, and no one has ever pointed out that each one of these faces looks more or less the same, and that similarity is also, by unlucky chance, shared by my client.'

But the police say that they can only work with the information that they have been given, and that if the suspect walks around wearing a 'bomber jacket and jeans' then he is asking to be arrested. Accompanying his client as they left Camden Police Station Mr Walton said, 'My client is an honest man who just happens to suffer from a rare facial disfigurement which makes his face look like an identikit photo. This is discrimination, pure and simple.'

As they walked down the steps of the station, the pair sighed wearily on hearing a returning police constable shouting, 'There he is! Quick, get him!'

The identikit scandal is the second setback to hit the Met this month. Two weeks ago, police were criticized for releasing an 'artist's impression' of a suspect without having checked whether or not the likeness was being done by a rubbish artist.

Emergency tracheotomies 'not as easy as they look on TV' 21 October

An inquiry in London today heard the evidence of a passenger who performed a mid-air tracheotomy on a fellow passenger who got into difficulty during a recent transatlantic flight.

Tom Belvedere, 43, who has no medical training, carried out the complex procedure on 29-year-old Suzanne Kirby. The operation, which involves making an incision into the windpipe and blowing air into the lungs, is only recommended as a last resort, if life is in danger.

'It wasn't easy, I can tell you,' said Tom. 'What with the turbulence and only a plastic knife and fork to cut with, it's a miracle she made it through. Thank heavens I am a fan of medical shows and I have seen it before. But those pros make it look easy. Getting the pen in was a right bastard! Messy as hell too.'

However, Mr James Knight, the consultant who treated Ms Kirby on the ground, was highly critical of the would-be doctor. 'It's always best to seek a qualified medical practitioner. It's also pretty important to make sure that the patient is actually in need of a life-saving operation before you go carving her up and sticking a tube in her throat. It's also not advisable to perform surgery when you are pissed.'

Mr Knight's comments came after the inquest heard evidence directly from the 'patient'. Speaking softly, the attractive Ms Kirby said that Mr Belvedere, who had been drinking throughout the flight, had been 'a bit too chatty' and 'bordering on the annoying'. She described how she coughed slightly and reached for some water, saying that she had something in her throat. 'The next thing I knew Mr Belvedere had picked me up and carried me to the back of the plane. He demanded brandy from the cabin crew which he sloshed on my neck. I was frozen in fear; thank God I passed out. When I woke up I was in hospital with real doctors, not that bloody clown.'

Mr Belvedere was arrested when he later turned up at the hospital in a doctor's coat for what he called his 'post-op rounds'. It turns out he also has a number of convictions for indecent assaults on cattle, dating back to when he was an avid viewer of *All Creatures Great and Small*.

MAN HIRES SECOND LIFE COACH

25 October

A north London man who had become dissatisfied with the way things were going for him in his virtual world of Second Life, has hired a life coach to help him find some meaning and direction in his internet-based alternative reality.

Phil Conrad, 33, had initially found that hours spent on Second Life had helped him escape from the problems of his marriage break-up, stalled career and lack of direction in life. He was making acquaintances online, earning Linden Dollars and developing a whole new successful existence. 'It was great; my Second Life persona was doing all the things I never did in reality – maybe because he was taller, richer and better looking. But recently, my Second Life just seems to have got stuck in a rut. My avatar is unmotivated and indecisive, I can't seem to stick at anything or focus on my goals. That's when I started seeing a Second Life coach.'

Every Thursday night at eight, Phil has been going online and meeting with his Second Life coach in the amazing residence he built himself during a more productive period. She helps him set some long-term goals and focus on what he wants from the virtual world. Last Thursday, however, Phil says his avatar 'just never got it together', and 'sort of stayed in doing nothing'.

'I got fed up with the coach,' he explained. 'Last week she was so full of clichés and platitudes; it was like: "Second Life is what you make it." And: "You only get out of Second Life as much as you put in." She even started going on about this whole other world called First Life, where you had to face up to your problems. She was just like the life coach I used to see in my normal life.'

115

Inter-faith strife to end following launch of the 'Wiki-Bible'

27 October

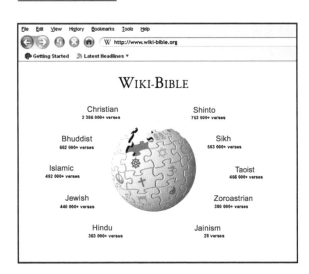

A new online user-generated concept from the creators of Wikipedia is hoping to end all religious strife across the world.

The so-called Wiki-Bible project plans to have one online holy book for all world faiths, written and edited by the worldwide community.

'Like all ideas, the genius is in its simplicity,' said creator Karl Eckstein. 'If someone feels strongly that the central tenet of another religion is fundamentally wrong, then they can go online and change it. This morning the Wiki-Bible stated quite categorically that there was but one God and his name was Allah. This afternoon, another editor had corrected that to explain that there were in fact a number of different gods including Ganesh, Krishna, Vishnu and Cristiano Ronaldo.'

It is hoped that by asserting their version of the one true faith, fundamentalists around the world will be diverted from asserting their beliefs through violence or religious persecution. 'But we hope that, eventually, people of all faiths will accept this as the one true holy text for all mankind,' added Eckstein. 'Plus if you find yourself having broken one of the central commandments of your religion, you can always go online and change it. This morning the seventh commandment read "Though shalt not commit adultery. Unless it is with thy neighbour's wife Janice."'

The Wiki-Bible site has been swamped with visitors since its launch, with thousands of editors from the Vatican, Israel and Mecca logging on to adjust the emphasis in the Wiki-Gospels. 'There are still a few nuances to be ironed out,' admitted Eckstein. 'I think that bit about God having promised the land of Judea to the Buddhists and Taoists as well might not be very helpful. And admittedly it all gets a bit confusing towards the end.' But according to the world's definitive holy e-book, for the time being the sacred text is quite clear. 'And yea, God laid down his life for his only son. And his name was Luke Skywalker.'

Vampires may target ladies with 'flimsy nightwear', warns police chief

30 October

Attractive young women with a predilection for flimsy, lace-based nightwear are being warned not to believe themselves safe from the attentions of vampires this Halloween.

The new warning comes despite assurances that Romanian workers will not be allowed into the country without work permits, as it is believed that some Transylvanian migrants may have already been slipping past passport control before the new ruling comes into force. 'With Romania joining the EU this is an increasing problem,' said Police Chief Sir Ian Blair. 'But known vampires are already entering this country in broad daylight. Well, not broad daylight, obviously, that's just a figure of speech.

'So at this time of year we are reminding young ladies who are inclined to swan around on balconies looking wistful or silhouetting themselves against dramatic skylines to take the usual precautions of holding up crucifixes and hanging up garlic. It's just common sense really.'

116

Suicide bomber sees himself 'more in a management role'

31 October

Iqbal Ibrahim, a newly recruited member of an al-Qaeda-linked group in Baghdad, is reported to be thrilled to have been selected to fulfil his dream of participating in the Jihad against Western troops in the country, but is a little disappointed that his first assignment – driving a car loaded with explosives into **the wall of the Green Zone – might not be the best use of his skills and abilities.**

'Don't get me wrong,' said the 21-year-old insurgent from his family home in the Baghdad suburbs, 'I'd do anything to have the American invaders out of our country and to create a true Islamic state in Iraq, and I'm delighted that the bosses want to give me so much responsibility so quickly . . . but I had been hoping for something in more of a supervisory capacity, so to speak.'

Ibrahim has now requested a meeting with the terror cell's leader to present some of his proposals for expanding the group and its international profile, with him in the role of an 'ideas man' responsible for 'long-term strategic thinking'. He also plans to highlight his PowerPoint skills and a Media Studies qualification, which he considers could be used to help the group communicate more effectively through its broadcast messages and video-recorded beheadings.

But in spite of his apparent reluctance to participate in the suicide attack, and rumours that he's under pressure from a fiancée angry at the prospect of his receiving seventy-two virgins, the young fundamentalist was adamant that the proposed strike should go ahead.

'It's not that I don't think this mission is important,' he insisted, 'but others may be better suited for this particular holy role. I have a cousin who, even when we were children together, was dedicated to identifying any possible little breach of scripture and would give me a well-deserved Chinese burn to help me remember each transgression. That kind of devotion to Islam deserves an opportunity like this. I happen to have his mobile number right here.'

Halloween party neither frightening nor fun

1 November

There was a disappointment in Guildford, Surrey, last night when a much anticipated Halloween fancy-dress party failed to be either scary or amusing.

Party-goer Steve Wellington had spent the week before carefully preparing his 'serial killer' costume and looking forward to what he hoped would be a spooky night of drunken entertainment. 'I had this image in my mind of everyone in outlandish, creative costumes but most people just turned up in their normal clothes with, like, a pirate hat or something, which they took off anyway.'

Wellington, one of three hockey-masked attendees, was also disappointed to discover a dearth of 'sexy costumes' such as slinky vampires or hot witches in fishnet stockings. 'One woman came in a nurse's costume, but she was actually a paediatric nurse who had just finished her shift.'

Mark Spelling, who came as 'someone from the eighties', bemoaned a combination of poor music and a lack of new people as the main contributing factor for the boredom. 'No one was in charge of the music. Once we got to the end of a CD there was a period of silence while whoever was sitting next to the stereo chose what to put on next. Apparently the host had done a special Halloween-themed playlist with songs like 'Thriller' and 'Monster Mash', but it finished before everyone arrived.'

Host Mandy Jones was unsure what the problem was: 'I don't understand. I had fake cobwebs everywhere and a cardboard skeleton on the front door. How could you fail to have a blast? Maybe next time I just won't build it up in my mind beforehand. Anyway, this year's New Year's party is going to be awesome!'

US JUDGE CENSURED FOR ISSUING DEATH PENALTY DRESSED IN HALLOWEEN COSTUME

2 November

A JUDGE IN THE UNITED STATES HAS BEEN OFFICIALLY REPRIMANDED FOR SENTENCING A MAN TO DEATH WHILE DRESSED IN A SKELETON COSTUME FOR HALLOWEEN.

'I don't know what all the fuss is about,' said Judge Carl Everett from Tallahassee, Florida. 'It was only a bit of fun to break up the monotony of what's been a very long trial. My mask wasn't very scary really, and I did take it off every now and then when it got a bit sweaty inside.'

Judges in the United States do not wear the formal robes and wigs that are traditional in Britain, but some legal commentators feel that the outfit may have been slightly too casual on this occasion. At Judge Everett's

New Sat Navs to feature 'Tourette's setting'

<u>3 November</u>

The latest satellite-navigation systems to hit the market come with a range of specialized new settings including 'Tourette's Syndrome Mode' for drivers who are not afraid to have their GPS tell it like it is.

The new generation of in-car navigation computers was unveiled by Jeremy Clarkson on *Top Gear*. Complaints jammed the BBC switchboard after the machine informed the presenter, 'Your final destination is two hundred yards on the left. Now go fuck yourself!' The rest of the programme was ruined by random shouts of 'Clarkson, you wanker!' although it turned out these were not coming from the GPS but one of the cameramen making the most of the opportunity.

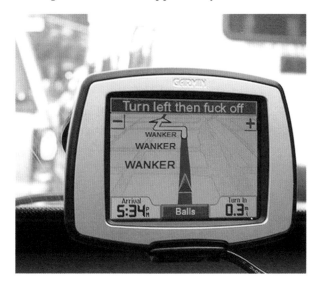

Bill Gates stuns the world with 'Cardigan 2009'

<u>4 November</u>

The computer world was thrilled and amazed this week when Bill Gates finally unveiled the long-awaited 'Cardigan 2009'.

It was the Microsoft CEO's first new knitwear in over eight years and is being heralded as the most advanced cardigan the softwear giant has ever developed.

'Today is a big day. This cardigan marks a new era in smart-casual for us,' Gates told the enthralled delegates. 'The double pockets can hold more parallel Biros than previous cardigans, and the combination of a zip and buttons makes this the most secure cardy I have ever worn. The sleeves can be pushed up in warmer weather and further security add-ons such as leather elbow patches can be purchased separately.'

---

suggestion, all the officials of the courtroom came to the final day of the trial dressed in scary costumes for Halloween.

'It was completely inappropriate,' said Defense Attorney Greg Anderton, who did not want to risk offending the judge by being a spoil-sport and so reluctantly came as Frankenstein's monster. 'He knew that the verdict and sentencing would probably fall on 31 October, but still made us all dress up as witches, vampires and Egyptian Mummies. The clerk of the court came

as a zombie and called me a party pooper, but I just don't think that is appropriate when someone is being given the death penalty.'

The case in question was that of a 37-year-old Hispanic man who was charged with the premeditated murder of his wife and her lover. The fatal injuries that had been described to the jury inspired one of them to come with blood-soaked bandages around his head as part of his Kurt Cobain costume. But another juror was reprimanded by the judge for not making enough

effort with her costume. 'Just wearing a pair of round spectacles doesn't make you Harry Potter,' he said during his summing up.

Inspired by events in the courtroom, the wardens on Florida's Death Row also dressed up, with the result that two prisoners were executed by officers in Halloween fancy dress. 'Perhaps we should have warned them beforehand, but seeing the Grim Reaper next to the electric chair is one way of learning that your last-minute appeal to the Governor has been turned down.'

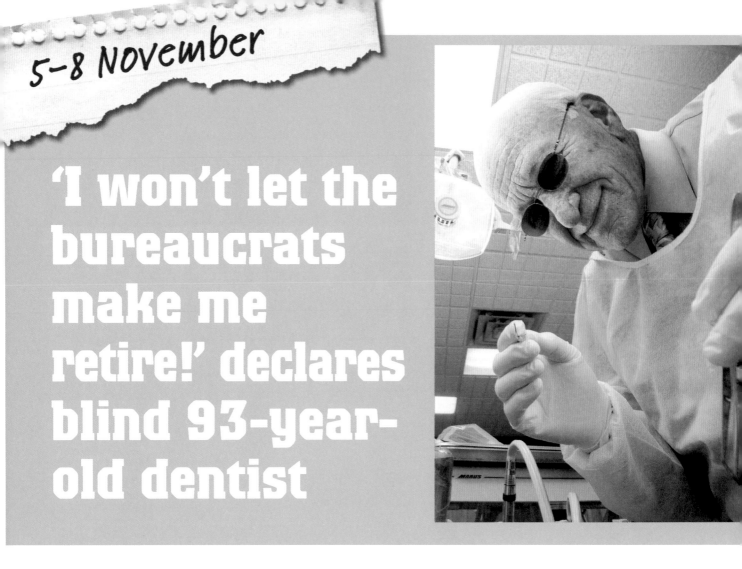

'I won't let the bureaucrats make me retire!' declares blind 93-year-old dentist

5 November

Friends and family of Britain's oldest dentist are claiming he is being discriminated against, after health officials urged 93-year-old Sidney Copeland to retire from dentistry due to his 'extremely shaky hands and total loss of vision in both eyes.'

'This is discrimination against the blind, pure and simple. I think that the way Dad keeps going is an inspiration to us all,' said his son David, through a rather ill-fitting brace. 'He is still out there, doing what he loves, and if these Brussels bureaucrats think they can stop him drilling, then they don't know my dad!'

But campaigners for the elderly are distancing themselves from the 93-year-old, who has continued to carry out complex dental work despite a number of complaints about wildly inaccurate drilling, massive loss of blood around the mouth and face and one incident in which a patient had a filling inserted into the middle of his forehead. 'I've been doing this job for so long, I know where all their teeth are anyway,' chirped a cheerful Mr Copeland, who hopes to become the world's oldest dentist. 'You've got to keep going, haven't you? Dentistry is all I know!'

Under European law, dentists are required to pass an eye test to ensure the accuracy of their work, and regular checks ensure that dental surgeons meet the rigorous safety standards expected of the industry. The most recent inspection of Mr Copeland's surgery reported grubby premises, the regular use of a Black & Decker drill and 'dental tools not being washed after being used to scrape cat food out of the tin'. But an anti-EC campaign on Mr Copeland's behalf by the *Daily Mail* fell away as a number of former patients complained that the elderly dentist had caused them immense pain, distress and disfigurement, and that his determination to keep working until he turns a hundred takes no account of the fact that he regularly drills through patients' front teeth, chins and, on one occasion, their shoulder blade.

'The Brussels bureaucrats have gone mad!' declared Mr Copeland. 'Is this what we want, some busy-body in Belgium telling us we can't drill people's teeth just because we don't happen to pass the latest blindness test that they've just dreamed up?' 'You tell them Dad!' said his son, who then broke off his press conference to pick up some pieces of his teeth that had fallen on to the carpet.

CITY TRADER AND RUGBY FAN APOLOGIZES FOR BLOCKING PUB TV SCREEN

7 November

City trader Fraser 'Diggers' Digby apologized to an elderly man on Saturday after he realized that he had briefly blocked his view of the rugby match on the pub TV screen.

'When I realized I had obscured this elderly gentleman's line of vision by standing in the middle of the pub clutching a pint and eating a large bap, I was mortified. Like all large, ex-public schoolboys who work in the City, I am constantly striving to be ultra-considerate to those around me. I would never talk loudly on a mobile phone if anyone could overhear me, stub out a cigar in an ashtray where another group of people were sitting or needlessly block the bar where people were trying to be served. That's just the way we are.' Fraser actually missed the end of the rugby international, when he was asked to move his BMW X5 which had blocked in two other vehicles in the pub car park. 'God, I am so sorry,' said the burly ex-Etonian and bond dealer. 'That is so totally unlike me.'

Parents to be notified if their children are working class

8 November

A new initiative from the Department of Children, Schools and Families will see parents notified by letter if their children are considered to be at risk of growing into working-class adults.

The controversial intervention follows a series of concerns about children eating unhealthy diets, not being encouraged to read at home, being allowed out late at night, breaking the law and generally appearing a bit unkempt or failing to wear a single item from Mini Boden.

Professor Sir Piers Cockburn (Oxon) warned that 'Unless steps are taken now, large numbers of our pupils could leave school unable to sustain a dinner-party conversation about the Tuscan countryside or the benefits of organic vegetables. The only circumstance in which children should be out late at night is if they are queuing up to buy the latest Harry Potter book dressed as a wizard.'

However, the idea has been slammed as 'nanny-state intervention gone mad' by some educationalists, who fear that schools will become stigmatized for not doing enough to encourage pupils to listen to *The Archers* or browse around antique shops in Richmond. 'Children are all different and we should accept that some may get the bus to school rather than be driven in a large people-carrier listening to storybook tapes,' said one teacher. 'Children mustn't be made to feel second class, just because they are going to be poor and exploited for the rest of their lives.'

The government has also revealed that it may publish league tables detailing the percentage of proletarian children in each school, so that parents can make informed choices before sending their children into an environment with kids who 'may have had fizzy drinks at breakfast'. But ministers have admitted that writing to working-class parents may not be that effective in the short term. 'We accept that they are unlikely to read any letters we send them anyway. We are thinking of putting a big warning on the side of crisp packets instead.'

Ford unveil new car for the clown market

9 November

The troubled Ford Motor Company this week unveiled the new Ford Coco: the long-awaited comedy car aimed at the lucrative clown market.

Ford are reported to be pinning all their hopes on this new model, aiming to become the brand leader in mid-range vehicles that backfire and then fall apart as they drive round and round in little circles. After years in the design stage and endless boardroom battles that saw Ford executives getting custard pies in the face, the clown car was finally unveiled at the Birmingham Motor Show. There were gasps and applause, but unfortunately very little

laughter. 'The car is fine,' said Mike Peters of *What Car*, 'but it hasn't overcome that fundamental design problem of all previous clown cars: it just isn't very funny.'

The specially hired clown drivers were keen to point out the many exciting new features, such as windscreen-washers aimed at the driver, the loud, old-fashioned 'parp-parp' horn and an emergency bucket of confetti to throw over fellow clowns. The official voiceover chuckled that 'The Ford Coco is a five-door – no, hang on, four-door! No, now only two-door, mid-range family vehicle that can do zero to three miles per hour in about four minutes!' And then one of the clowns pretended to cry when the steering wheel came off in his hand. But by this time the straight-faced crowd had drifted off to look at other exhibits.

ISLE OF WIGHT TO GET CEEFAX

10 November

Residents of the Isle of Wight are excited that the information revolution is about to hit the island with the arrival of the BBC's up-to-the-minute information service Ceefax.

```
CEEFAX 1    100 Thu 11 Jul
BBC CEEFAX
Cowes West News
OAP SCOOTER STOLEN BY HOODY 161
Cowes East News
WOMAN, 87, DIES              162

A-Z INDEX        199  NEWS HEADLINES    101
BBC INFO         695  NEWS FOR REGION   160
CHESS            568  NEWSROUND         570
COOKERY          560  RADIO        BBC1 640
COMMUNITY BBC2   650  READ HEAR    BBC2 640
```

By pressing different coloured buttons on their television remote controls, local residents will be able to get instant weather and travel information, recipes, horoscopes and more.

'I can't believe that the information revolution can go any further than this,' said Arnold Harrison, 76.

DESCENDENTS OF SLAVE TRADE APOLOGIZE FOR RAP

<u>11 November</u>

The government's apology for Britain's involvement in the slave trade finally brought a reaction from Britain's Afro-Caribbean community today, who responded with a full apology for the suffering endured as a result of rap music.

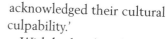

'We cannot continue to ignore the incalculable misery that has been caused by people having to listen to rap music, a genre which we must acknowledge originated within the black community,' said Kofi Owusu, the editor of *Black Nation Quarterly*. 'Millions of Britons, black and white, have had to endure this shouty tuneless nonsense and it is time that black people

acknowledged their cultural culpability.'

With both sides of Britain's racial divide doing their utmost to appear conciliatory following the bicentenary of the abolition of slavery, the apologies went back and forth throughout the day. The Prime Minister also apologized for the vaguely offensive 1970s sitcom *Love Thy Neighbour* and the fact that the black Labrador in *The Dam Busters* is called 'Nigger'. The head of the Commission for Racial Equality then issued a statement saying that the annoying fashion in which trousers were far too baggy and hung down around the wearers' crotch also originated in the black community and for this he expressed 'very sincere regret'. Ten Downing Street issued a further statement saying sorry for the enamel golliwog badges you used to get with Robertson's jam, for the original words of 'Eeny-Meeny-Miny-Mo' and for Phil Collins's cover version of 'You Can't Hurry Love'.

The debate eventually fell apart in confusion when both sides attempted to apologize for Michael Jackson.

BELGIUM DEAD;
LAY UNDISCOVERED FOR TWO WEEKS

12 November

The UN today officially announced that Belgium has died. The discovery was made when Germany called round one afternoon to investigate an unpleasant smell drifting across the border and found the curtains still drawn.

The UN did acknowledge that Belgium hadn't shown up at meetings for a fortnight but claimed that nobody noticed. 'It didn't really say too much when it was here, didn't have many friends – or enemies either. And it never socialized. However, Austria did mention that stocks of hand-made chocolates and Stella Artois had dropped a bit, which should have been a warning sign.'

Next-door neighbours France commented: 'Belgium kept itself pretty much to itself really, didn't come and go too much, a fairly quiet type.'

The last will and testament will be read next month and is expected to be uncontested, with the Flemish region going to the Netherlands and the Walloon region being given to France. The only contentious issue concerns the port of Ostend, with Germany claiming it was promised the busy shipping port by Belgium some time ago. 'We could send troops in,' said Berlin, 'but it ended up causing all kinds of fuss last time.'

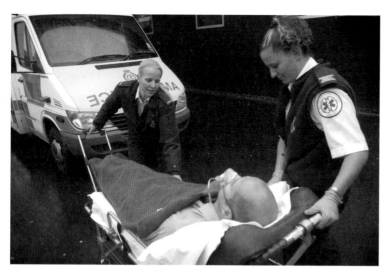

NHS to launch 'Intensive Care in the Community'

13 November

The Government is extending the controversial 'Care in the Community' programme to include 'Intensive Care in the Community'.

With NHS bills spiralling and a growing shortage of beds, the Department of Health announced that the new scheme would enable desperately ill patients to begin to reintegrate with society while they were still lying unconscious attached to a life-support machine.

The first Intensive Care in the Community patients were wheeled out of St Thomas' Hospital and relocated in a nearby neighbourhood reintegration project in the heart of the capital. However, critics of the new scheme say that it is purely a cost-cutting exercise and that the quality of intensive care suffers when patients end up being parked underneath railway arches or abandoned on park benches. During the night a number of charities such as the Salvation Army found themselves not only providing accommodation but also performing emergency life-saving operations on people they had found left outside the hospital on trolleys.

Junior Health Minister Jennifer Craster said the government is keen to develop a less interventionist approach to modern medicine. 'With patients stuck inside, wired up to all sorts of intrusive machines, they are inevitably going to get depressed. How much better that they are out in the fresh air and the sunshine where we can let the wonderful human body recover the wholly natural way?'

One doctor, however, remained sceptical: 'The human body does have a "wholly natural" means of responding to serious illness,' he said. 'It's called "death".'

YOUNG PERSON ATTENDS ROCK CONCERT WITHOUT ATTEMPTING TO RECORD ENTIRE EVENT ON MOBILE PHONE

14 November

Musical history was made this week at the Hammersmith Apollo when a pop fan went to see Lily Allen in concert and kept her mobile phone in her pocket for the entire duration of the show.

While all around her were holding up their camera phones to get a blurred picture of Lily in the distance or were recording the distorted sound of fans singing along, Emma Jenkins opted simply to enjoy the experience in the present moment.

'I just decided that the sound quality would probably be better on the Lily Allen CD I had at home,' said Emma, 15. 'And that I could get better photos off the internet, and that the video quality on my little Nokia is on balance not as good as all the stuff on MTV that's produced by professional video directors.'

Badgers to be sent to Iraq

15 November

British badgers will be sent to serve with UK forces in Iraq under plans unveiled jointly by the Ministry of Defence and Defra today.

For some time Britain has been seeking a credible exit strategy that would allow troops to return home without accusations that the British government was abandoning the war-torn region. It is hoped that a token presence of British nocturnal carnivores will go some way towards countering allegations of 'cut and run', while simultaneously mollifying UK farmers' demands for action against badgers back at home.

'British badgers will play their part in supporting American and Iraqi forces as they establish the fragile democracy in Baghdad,' said a government spokesman yesterday. 'As we are now handing over control of the country to the Iraqi people, the badgers' duties will not extend to flying reconnaissance missions, driving armoured vehicles or guarding key installations. Their role will be more focused on scurrying around at night snuffling out worms and stag beetles.'

Soviet Union to re-form for 'one night only'

16 November

The countries of the former Soviet Union have agreed to re-form for a special one-off evening of military posturing, human-rights abuse and state-controlled oppression.

The fifteen countries stretching from Lithuania to Tajikistan were persuaded to bury their differences and get back together to cash in on the current trend for 1970s nostalgia.

Ukraine, the country that first mooted the idea of the 'Soviet Re-Union', said last night, 'We never thought it would really happen, but when we started talking to each other the old memories came flooding back and we realized we owed it to the fans.'

Belarus agreed, saying: 'It's great to be free, independent and democratic, but we can't deny we had some good times together and it'll be great to see the others after all this time and feel part of that huge terrifying Soviet power bloc – even if it's for just one night!'

All the members have been digging out their old furry hats and hammer-and-sickle badges and practising their lines about glorious tractor production. Promoters were wary of backing the reunion until Russia finally came on board. Despite what Kyrgyzstan claimed about the Soviet Union being a team of equals, as one fan said, 'The Soviet Union without Russia would have been like the Osmonds without Donny.'

Russia was finally persuaded to take part in the reunion after promises that it would be allowed to bully the smaller nations. The planned reunion looked in danger last night, however, when the re-formed Soviet Union encountered a number of unforeseen copyright problems. 'We'd been planning to do all the old favourites like "Destabilizing the Middle East" or "Invading Afghanistan". Trouble is, some bastard's gone and nicked our act!'

NATIONAL CURRICULUM TO INCLUDE 'BLEEDIN' OBVIOUS'

17 November

The Department of Education has announced that it is widening the National Curriculum to include lessons in the Bleedin' Obvious.

Research has shown that much of Britain's workforce is undereducated in this area, and continues to fall for email scams, *Reader's Digest* appeals and offers of extended warranties.

'In the modern global economy Britain's workforce needs to be highly skilled and educated,' said Junior Education Minister Sarah Beaumont. 'Frankly, if we've still got people thinking that they really are the millionth visitor to a certain website, then there really isn't much hope for any of us.'

Lessons in the Bleedin' Obvious will also explain that being rude to a policeman who has pulled you over for a driving offence will not result in a quick resolution of the matter or smaller fine, nor is it generally worth making jokes about bombs and terrorism to airport security staff.

Pupils will be taught that if they get seriously into debt with the bank, then paying it off by borrowing lots of money from that dodgy bloke on the estate may not be the end of all their problems. Another lesson includes learning what happens if you try and clear the compacted grass cuttings off the lawn-mower blade while it is still connected to the mains.

'It's great to get proper training in the Bleedin' Obvious before we head out to the workplace,' said sixteen-

year-old Simon Jonson. 'I've seen a really well-paid job I want to apply for that will let me work from home. It was advertised on a bit of paper tied on to a lamppost so it must be from a very reputable source.'

127

Ulster mural painters 'angry over peace process'

18 November

Angry artists in Derry and Belfast have laid down their brushes in protest at the lack of masked heroes, violent clashes and hunger-striking prisoners to portray.

The house-high murals traditionally reflect the years of struggle and turmoil that have afflicted the area. However, since the advent of peace and democratic accountability following the Good Friday agreement ten years ago, many of the artists have had to find alternative employment. One artist recounted how he tried to get a job as a designer with Clinton Cards, 'but they said there was a limited market for birthday cards featuring masked youths throwing petrol bombs.'

The painters claim to be forgotten victims of the peaceful political solution to Northern Ireland's problems. In Derry's Bogside there are many murals depicting the horror of the massacre of unarmed civilians by British paratroopers on Bloody Sunday. One muralist asked, 'Where will the future inspiration for artists come from? Quite frankly, the image of Ian Paisley and Gerry Adams sharing a joke and a chocolate digestive does nothing to inspire.'

The mural painters are organizing a march in the hope that it might provide some more inspiration. 'What we need is for the protest to turn ugly, with perhaps some unprovoked violence from the security forces and maybe a pointless death or two. We're all keeping our fingers crossed.'

HELLO! PUBLISHES DIANA COLONOSCOPY PHOTOS

19 November

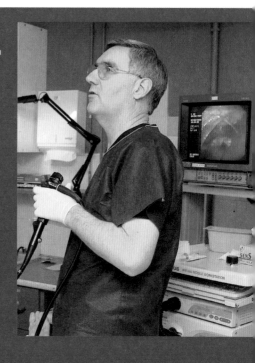

Hello! magazine is to publish intimate photos of Diana, Princess of Wales, taken during a colonoscopy that she had one week before her fatal car crash. The release of the images of the Princess's internal examination was justified as being 'of immense interest' to all those who loved the People's Princess, even though members of the Spencer family were critical that such private shots were being allowed into the public domain.

Although it cannot be discerned from the photos, Diana was wearing a green hospital gown with easy-tie strings, which was later auctioned for one of her charities. Royal watchers say the intimate pictures reveal a warm, hidden, more private side to the Princess, 'though her coy beauty remains unmistakable'.

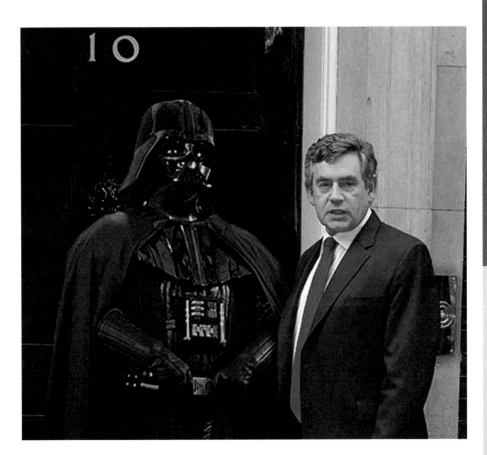

Gordon Brown has Darth Vader to tea at Downing Street

20 November

Prime Minister Gordon Brown has been criticized by Jedi supporters for inviting Dark Lord of the Sith Darth Vader to tea at 10 Downing Street.

Looking older and frailer, the former ruler of the Galactic Empire posed with the Prime Minister outside 10 Downing Street yesterday before going inside to discuss 'a range of domestic and galactic issues'.

The move has angered more traditional supporters of the Labour Party, who still have bitter memories of the brutal enforcement of Vader's rule throughout the galaxy during the 1980s. But the new Labour Prime Minister insisted that he had always been an admirer of Darth Vader's toughness and resolute approach, although as a security precaution the Dark Lord was not permitted to take his light sabre into Number 10. It also emerged that a pre-emptive attempt at even-handedness had backfired when an earlier invitation to key Jedi supporters had to be withdrawn after R2-D2 and C-3P0 failed to get through the Downing Street metal detector.

Despite sounding increasingly breathless and wheezy, Darth Vader was keen to discuss his meeting with the Prime Minister and share a surprising twist with waiting reporters. 'Gordon Brown is not my enemy,' he announced. 'He is my son.'

SKY TO LAUNCH 'UK HOSTAGE' CHANNEL

22 November

Sky Television has announced plans to add to its extensive programme choice with a new channel dedicated exclusively to terrorist hostages.

Sky claimed to have signed exclusive deals with all the major terror organizations and their factions, while Dermot O'Leary has been approached to do studio-based interviews with the hostages' families. 'Yeah, we want Dermot to do: how are they feeling? How would the hostage react in this situation? Any embarrassing stories from childhood? That type of thing.'

The channel will be officially launched next month, pending a possible legal action from the producers of *I'm a Celebrity . . . Get Me Out of Here!*, who had plans to drop Tara Palmer-Tomkinson in Gaza and just see what happened.

SKY uk hostage news

where are they now?
what are they wearing?
how's their hair?

GOVERNMENT TO INTRODUCE GCSE IN TEXTING

24 November

In a bold move to re-engage teenagers with their education and raise the rate of GCSE passes, the Department of Education are introducing a new GCSE course, Texting, from next September.

'Kids are already taking their mobiles into their GCSEs and texting each other all the answers,' said a spokesman for the Department of Education. 'This is just heading into the problem.' Although the pass rate is expected to be high, students who fail the course will be notified by text message: 'U hv fld ur GCSE – soz :-('

If the GCSE in texting is a success, then further new exams will be rolled out in 2009. These include Proficiency in Internet-Based Social Interaction, or Beboing, and Urban Interaction in the Community, which is basically Mucking about in Shopping Centres and Calling Any Adult Who Tells You Off a Paedo.'

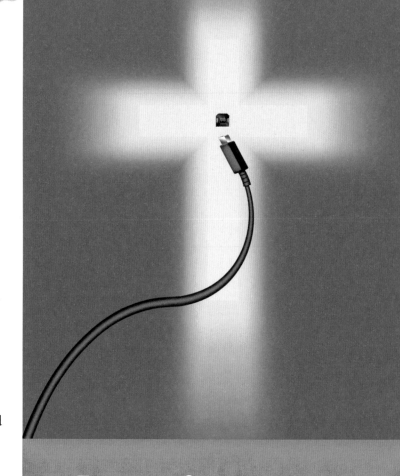

The Bible: Testament 3.0 leaked on the internet

28 November

Extracts from the eagerly awaited book *The Bible: Testament 3.0* filled the internet last week, and several websites posted what appeared to be copies of the complete manuscript, which has been kept in a tightly sealed cave of secrecy leading up to its Sunday release.

Eager fan Archbishop Rowan Williams downloaded a copy of the wildly anticipated threequel and revealed details in his Sunday sermon. 'Without giving too much away,' he preached, 'I can confirm rumours that a major character is killed off about halfway through the book. However, he comes back to life again before disappearing for several years, and after a triumphant return he dies again, rises from the dead and once again disappears with a promise to return later.'

The new book, which has been dubbed 'the most exciting yet', will feature all the thrills and spills of the first two testaments, including walking on water, flying and water-to-wine magic. Jesus Christ and his twelve friends will also encounter a host of new sins to tempt them, including smoking in a public building, using a mobile phone when driving and many old favourites such as betrayal, adultery and ox-coveting.

Catastrophes including floods, locusts and Chris Moyles will hinder the thirteen friends on their quest, and fans will be pleased to note that old adversary the Devil will return, this time as an elusive Afghan terrorist.

If the online material is genuine, it would represent a major breach of security that God Inc. has been working feverishly to protect. The publishers of the blockbuster fantasy series released a statement saying, 'Thou shalt not read our book on thy internet', at which lots of excited fans were alerted to the fact that it was on the internet.

Pool full of teenagers fail to react as very fat man goes for a swim

30 November

A Milton Keynes man was left shocked and dismayed yesterday afternoon when a swimming pool full of teenagers failed to produce a single joke or derogatory remark about his excessive weight.

Mr David Blunden had been warned that he was 'dangerously overweight' and could be classed as 'obese' and so had gone to the Plaza pool fully expecting to be taunted from the very moment he put on his XXXL trunks.

But although it was the school holidays and the pool was full of teenagers, the adolescents seemed unconcerned by the enormous rolls of bare flesh hanging over Mr Blunden's trunks as he paraded up and down the side of the pool. 'Fair play to him,' said Candice, aged 15. 'We just presumed he must have some sort of dietary or thyroid disorder, but respected him as he was endeavouring to do something about it.'

Pensioners offered chance to hibernate

2 December

The government has hit on a novel way to save money this Christmas, by offering pensioners the opportunity to hibernate for the next three or four months.

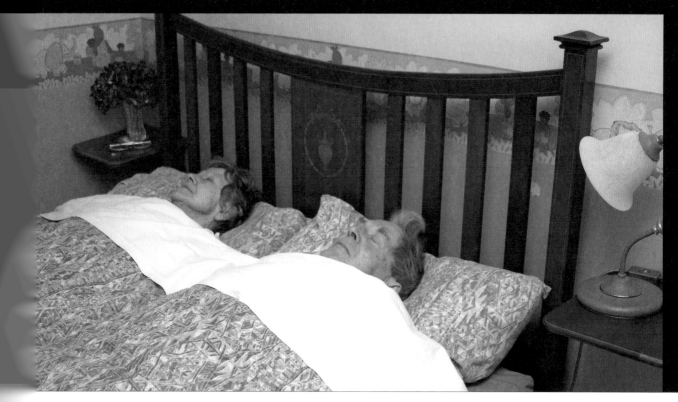

Significant savings are expected on pensions, flu jabs and winter fuel allowances if the pilot scheme is successful.

'Winter is a very difficult time for old people,' explained Junior Health Minister Karen Brady. 'Many die of flu, some slip on ice and break a hip, others are expected to visit relatives for Christmas and are distressed to see their grandchildren playing Grand Theft Auto or enjoying the overt homosexual references on the *Little Britain* DVD. Now they have the chance to skip all that, going to sleep in December and waking up in time to enjoy the daffodils.'

The NHS hibernation scheme is being piloted in Worthing, Sussex, where if it is successful, around 90 per cent of all local residents will be going to sleep for the next three months. Participants are given a nourishing milky drink, which contains sleep-inducing drugs, and are then tucked up in bed with the Teasmade set for April. Health visitors will tiptoe in once a week to feed the goldfish and

ensure that the electric blanket hasn't been left on.

But civil liberties groups have criticized the scheme, saying that many old people are being given the drugs by their families without knowing that they will be missing months of their life. One anonymous family confessed they had forced the drink on their elderly relative: 'This is great, we won't have to visit her for months,' said the victim's son-in-law. 'We've already got the kids' cash for Christmas off her; now we can put her in a coma and we won't have to listen to all that bloody moaning about "queers" getting married or "blacks" reading the news.'

The Health Minister said they were listening carefully to all the objections to the pilot hibernation scheme, and that all these issues would be discussed as a matter of urgency by a Parliamentary inquiry, which the government had entrusted to the House of Lords. However, work on the Lords' investigation appears to have been postponed until mid-May.

MAN WHO TRIED TO CARVE OUT HIS OWN ROUTE THROUGH IKEA STORE 'SO VERY SORRY'

6 December

A man who was trapped in the Thurrock branch of IKEA for almost seven hours yesterday spoke today of his deep regret at having ignored the strict arrow-based system for navigating the store.

Mike Brenman, 37, from Braintree, had been to the furnishing store many times before, and analysts believe this may have contributed to his over-confidence in going 'off-road'.

'I did see the arrows on the floor but I only went in for a deckchair and a garlic-crusher, so I thought it would be OK to try and cut across departments. But I just ended up back in the same place about twelve times. I see now how foolish my actions were, and I'm so very sorry for any distress caused to others, particularly my son who had opted to wait in the car.'

Dr Pepper 'has no genuine medical qualifications'

8 December

The moral integrity of soft-drink giant Schweppes was called into question today after it emerged that Dr Pepper is not a real doctor, has never been to medical school or received any form of health training, and has been using the title under false pretences.

Shampoo scientists awarded Nobel Prize

10 December

Scientists from cosmetics company L'Oréal were said to be 'shocked and delighted' today after being awarded the Nobel Prize for science.

The group, led by chief researcher Bob Mulligan, was chosen for its 'fresh and revolutionary insights into twenty-first century haircare' and was given a special mention for its brave research into how to deal with 'rebellious fly-away low pH hair and how obscure chemicals can apparently make your hair all shimmery and stuff like that'.

Industry insiders commented that although recent years have seen massive advances in shampoo technology, L'Oréal is widely considered to be the market leader, having created innovative active ingredients such as Pro-Retinol A, Ceramide R, and Pro-Cellulose Revitalift Epsilon, all of which are scientifically proven to possibly improve your hair's 'zesty shininess' by up to a maximum of 30 per cent or more.

Converted loft used to store stuff that used to be in loft

12 December

A London couple that spent £35,000 converting their loft to a spare bedroom are currently unable to use their new living space for all the boxes of junk being stored there.

'We always thought that the house could use an extra bedroom,' said Mark Campbell-Jones from Fulham, 'and eventually we decided to take out a bank loan and go for it.' The couple hired an architect, applied for planning permission from the local authority, got various estimates from local builders and finally cleared out all the junk that had piled up in their dusty old loft over the years.

'After months of builders and thirty-five grand later, the new spare bedroom looked fantastic,' said Mr Campbell-Jones. 'It was light and airy with views over London. The only problem was that we had to find somewhere to put all the boxes of stuff that we hadn't been able to throw out, and the top of the house seemed the obvious place.'

'Hilarious' YouTube clip not actually that funny

14 December

A clip on YouTube turned out to be not quite as hilarious as was promised this week.

Alan Toynbee, 27, from Swansea, spent the best part of Thursday evening telling his wife's brother about 'this absolutely bloody brilliant and hilarious' clip he had spotted on YouTube recently. But when the pair went over to Alan's computer and watched the clip they discovered it wasn't actually funny at all, just a rather annoying American teenager miming along to Depeche Mode's 'Master and Servant' with a hand-puppet.

'We sat in absolute silence for about four minutes, getting more and more embarrassed as we attempted but failed to laugh,' said Alan's brother-in-law Tony, 36. Alan's wife, who had apparently had six glasses of Pinot Grigio, arrived at the end of the clip and began giggling uncontrollably. 'That's not the clip,' Alan explained. 'That's just my screensaver.'

Gift solutions to feature 'Oh, that'll do' stickers

15 December

Leading department stores are making Christmas shopping easier this year by adding guidance stickers for vaguely appropriate Christmas gifts.

The new coding system enables shoppers to quickly evaluate the value and apparent 'thought' that has gone into each present so that customers can make the right choices for family and friends. Labels include: 'Oh that'll do', 'Sort of in the right area' and 'Appropriateness will need to be explained after opening'. The labels have already been stuck on a large number of Christmas gift ideas in major department stores and have been broadly welcomed by busy shoppers. Jenny Carter from Birmingham said, 'I was trying to think what to get for my brother in Germany who has never sent me so much as a card and suddenly saw this sticker on Jeffrey Archer's *Prison Diary* that said "It's shit, but it's all he deserves". It was perfect.'

One of the commonest stickers is 'Understandable but pointless'. A DVD about the year 1974, to be given to someone born in that year, may look like a personal gift that has involved a bit of thought and foreknowledge from the giver, but in fact it is actually a very dull and meaningless present that automatically qualifies for the 'Understandable but pointless' sticker. Similarly a sticker that says 'You know she'll take this back, but it'll look like you tried' is featured on a variety of ladies' clothes. At the very bottom of the range are gifts marked 'Just plain wrong'; these stickers are for VHS films to give to people you know only have a DVD player.

Jeff Napier-Johnson of the Retail Association claimed: 'The new gift-labelling system has resulted in far fewer people wandering around looking completely perplexed – and we may extend the idea next year. Shoppers themselves will be interviewed as they enter the store, and then will wear lapel stickers to guide our assistants: 'Rich but in a hurry', 'Mean and possibly light-fingered' and 'Stupid enough to take out the extended warranty'.

'Disillusioned' Mr Google resigns

16 December

Ken Google, whose hard work and long hours made him a household name to the worldwide online community, has resigned from single-handedly running the Google search engine, citing 'overwork and increasing disillusion with the public use of the internet' as his reasons.

Mr Google, 43, had been the power behind the 'www. google.com' website since 2001. 'It started as a bit of a hobby, but it just got out of hand,' he explained. Ken often found himself working twenty-three-hour shifts from his one-bedroom flat in Stafford town centre looking things up at lightning speed in an extensive collection of encyclopaedias, dictionaries and 1960s 'I-Spy' handbooks. 'I used to get a real buzz out of being the most efficient person on the net,' he said this morning. 'Terry Yahoo and I used to have this friendly rivalry going, and we'd meet every other Friday for a couple of pints at the King's Arms and discuss some of our favourite searches.

'But it got a bit more than I could cope with. And there are only so many times you can put together the possible links for "Pamela Anderson" and "Bosoms".'

The Google brand name will continue without Ken, although he was always so busy answering internet enquiries that he never took the trouble to establish ownership of the brand. 'But I did have the foresight to stipulate that if anyone ever wanted to use my name without me, they would have to pay me three hundred pounds. Clever, eh?'

Veteran tomato-tin denter retires

17 December

A tomato-canning factory in Modena, Italy, today bade farewell to one of its longest-serving employees.

Giuseppe Perona has been denting tins at the factory for thirty-seven years and stifled a tear as he said, 'It has been my life.'

INFANT CAROL SINGERS BOOED FOR 'BEING RUBBISH'

21 December

The festive spirit was in short supply in the Arndale Centre, Manchester, this weekend when a group of infant-school children singing Christmas carols were booed and heckled out of the shopping centre because they were so awful.

Arndale manager Sharon Hastings had thought it would be a nice touch to have local children sing traditional carols to put shoppers in the Christmas mood. So a class of six- and seven-year-olds from St Jerome's Infant School, Wythenshawe, lined up in front of the big Christmas tree looking 'sweet and angelic'. Shoppers stopped and smiled and waited for the singing to begin. Unfortunately, the standard was well below what everybody was expecting. 'Bloody hell, I've never heard "Away in a Manger" sung so badly,' said a mother of two. 'Frankly these kids were shite at singing and needed telling so.'

Some onlookers were prepared to give the young children the benefit of the doubt and waited for the next carol. But 'Little Donkey' was an even bigger disaster and soon the crowd began booing and slow handclapping. By the time they got on to 'Silent Night', people were shouting, 'I wish it was silent!', 'Shut up!' or 'You're shit!'

One or two of the children began to cry, but unfortunately this didn't stop the others from ploughing on with the dreadful caterwauling and eventually security guards came over and told the children and their teacher to 'sling their hook as they weren't welcome'.

Their teacher said she was appalled by the behaviour of the shoppers: 'These children are six and seven years old, and it took enormous courage for them to get up and sing in front of strangers. I can't believe how heartless and cruel everyone was. They were right though. The kids really were shit.'

AFRICAN VILLAGERS FED UP WITH GIFTS OF GOATS; WOULD RATHER JUST HAVE THE CASH

23 December

Villagers in sub-Saharan Africa have asked if well-meaning Westerners could desist from sending them 'useful' gifts this Christmas, such as farm animals, teaching materials and agricultural equipment, and have asked if it would be all right if they just had the money instead.

'I do not wish to sound ungrateful,' said Papa N'Diaye from the Senegalese village Ker Simbara, 'but we got a goat last year, and the year before. This Christmas could we maybe have an Xbox or even just the cash equivalent?'

But Oxfam's regional representative in the area was eager to explain the philosophy behind useful agricultural Christmas presents. 'There's a saying that we put on all our literature: "Give a man a fish and you feed him for a day. But give a man a fishing rod . . ."'

'And he turns into a boring twat,' chipped in one of the villagers.

Queen's Christmas speech; star storms out

25 December

Queen Elizabeth II stormed off the set of her official broadcast this morning shouting that she refused to work with 'fucking amateurs' and that they 'could get some other mug to do their crappy Christmas show for them'.

The Queen's official Christmas broadcast to the United Kingdom and Commonwealth has been a traditional highlight of the royal calendar dating

back to Her Majesty's first radio broadcast as monarch in 1952. However, in recent years television directors have found Her Majesty increasingly difficult to handle.

'I should have seen the warning signs when we got back her amended contract,' said top TV director John Stroud. 'There was a clause demanding two crates of lager in the dressing room and that one of the mirrors be laid out horizontally.'

But the real problems started when the crew began filming. The Queen accused the cameraman of making her 'look old' and said the whole approach was all 'yawn-yawn bloody talking heads again'. Various alternative ideas were discussed but the director tactfully suggested that the sketches and songs that the Queen had brought along were not quite ready for a wider audience. 'Her material was obscene,

to be honest,' said Stroud, 'really hardcore and totally unbroadcastable. It was all "fucking Brown" this and "that bitch Diana" that. It was just a drunken rant.'

The Queen had been swigging from a bottle of Jack Daniel's and was becoming increasingly aggressive as the morning wore on. After a twelfth take of the original formal script, the Queen finally snapped, threw a punch at a sound technician and stormed out.

BBC chiefs met in emergency session this morning to try and decide what to do this year, finally hitting on a formula that will keep the TV audience happy without trying to get the Queen back into the studio. One insider revealed, 'We have decided just to stick out last year's Christmas speech again. Frankly, we'll be surprised if anyone notices.'

Golfer stunned by useful Christmas present <u>26 December</u>

Keen golfer Tony Beckinsale was still in shock this morning the day after having received a high-quality and useful Christmas present.

Friends and relations of Mr Beckinsale have always found it easy to buy him Christmas presents owing to his well-known enthusiasm for the sport of golf. 'Last year I got him some novelty woollen hats to put on the ends of his golf clubs,' said his wife Cindy. 'His mother got him a brightly coloured golfing jumper, and then there were the musical golf balls, illuminating tees, porcelain golfing figures as well as all the comedy books recounting amusing anecdotes from the nineteenth hole!' But this year Tony Beckinsale only got one golf-related present: a box containing just twelve high-quality Titleist golf balls.

Tony fainted with shock, banged his head on the coffee table and is now recovering from concussion in Stepping Hill Hospital. Sadly doctors have said he won't be able to play golf for at least a year. 'He'll have to take up something less active like bridge,' said his wife. 'Luckily that's given me all sorts of new birthday present ideas: tea towels with the rules of bridge on, mugs with pictures of playing cards and novelty scoring cards . . .'

Essex criminals slam 'rubbish dog fight'

27 December

An illegal and vicious dog-fighting ring in Essex has folded after inexperienced criminals attempted to set up the ring using golden retriever puppies.

Romford police arrested seven suspects yesterday and removed a large quantity of dog-fighting paraphernalia, including six spiked dog collars, dog bowls labelled 'Killer', 'Psycho' and 'Tyson', and six cute puppies with a quantity of extra-soft toilet tissue.

Police believe Andrex puppies were only used because the organizers were inexperienced and ignorant of the various fighting breeds banned under the Dangerous Dogs Act. One of the seized 'dog fight' videos shows the ringleader, "Knuckles" Naylor, putting two puppies into an improvised fighting pit and then urging them on with cries of 'Get him, boy', 'Hold him, Psycho!' and

'Tear him! Tear him up good!' As the puppies gambol happily around the ring and frolic with some toilet paper, voices are heard saying, 'Why ain't they fighting?' and 'I don't think this is how it's supposed to work, you know. Maybe we should try Labrador puppies instead?'

'We've never come across gangs using eight-week-old golden retrievers,' said Detective Hooper of the Essex police. 'This gang was trying to organize illegal gambling on which dog would tear the other apart, but the scam failed when the little puppies just licked their brothers' and sisters' noses and then fell asleep across each other in an adorable pose.'

The gang is now in custody after police tracked down the 'mastermind' of the whole operation at his mansion outside Chingford. They entered the property despite the gangster warning them: 'Take one more step and I'll set my kittens on you.'

Old person sends letter without gold address sticker on the back

29 December

Postal workers on the Isle of Wight were shocked today to discover an envelope posted on the island that did not have a little label with the sender's address stuck carefully on the reverse side.

The Isle of Wight has a high proportion of pensioners and is proud to be home to Britain's most careful letter-writers. 'Any envelopes that are incorrectly addressed can always

be easily returned to sender,' said chief sorting officer Sarah Beaumont. 'Sometimes they're too mean to buy those little gold ones and they just use those free ones you get from the Woodland Trust or the RSPB.'

But now there are fears that Isle of Wight letter-writers might start throwing caution to the wind. 'It was like the crazy old lady just didn't care,' said Ms Beaumont. 'It was like she was saying, "I'm just going to post this letter and if they can't find the right place . . . what the hell, I'll just have to

live with the consequences." It's scary and dangerous, but there's something attractively compelling about people who live on the edge like that.'

Despite concerns, the letter arrived safely at its destination and the order for new address stickers was quickly dispatched.

Fire brigade turned up late to burning pizza shop 'as satirical statement'

31 December

Firefighters who turned up deliberately late to a burning pizza delivery company were reprimanded yesterday for making an ironic comment on their standard of service.

ProntoPizza of Balham, south London, was burnt to the ground back in June despite being less than half a mile from Balham fire station. When the flames initially broke out in the kitchen on a busy Friday evening, the manager Peter Annal immediately called 999 and requested the fire brigade. But fifteen minutes later, with the inferno spreading to the shop front and the upstairs rooms, the pizza chefs and delivery drivers were surprised to see a florist suddenly arrive with a bunch of flowers.

'This big burly bloke came with a load of lilies and violets. He was clearly a fireman but he said he was delivering the wedding bouquet we had ordered. It was like he was suppressing the giggles the whole time.'

Mr Annal urgently explained that he had in fact ordered a couple of fire engines and the fireman apologized and said he'd have to go back to the station. Thirty-five minutes later, with much of the downstairs now completely gutted, the fireman returned with a complete Ocado shopping delivery.

'It was then that one of our drivers recognized him,' explained Mr Annal. 'He said that he often delivered pizzas to him at the fire station, and that the firemen had been repeatedly irritated by late and incorrect orders.' A desperate Mr Annal then called the local police station who listened to what had happened. The police sent round a window cleaner, a central-heating engineer and some cold garlic bread.

'A number of fire engines did finally turn up about three hours after we had first called them,' said Mr Annal, 'but by then the whole building had burnt to the ground. And one of them kept saying, "Sooo sorry we didn't listen to what you actually asked for. We really must listen more carefully next time . . ."'

Yesterday at South London Magistrates' Court, six members of the Balham fire crew were found guilty of gross negligence and ordered by the judge to pay appropriate compensation. They were ordered to pay the pizza company a £1 voucher for taking longer than thirty minutes.

Picture Credits

About NewsBiscuit

The stories contained within these pages first appeared on NewsBiscuit in the two years following its launch in September 2006, during which time it quickly established itself as Britain's leading satirical website. Hundreds of thousands of readers from around the globe now log on every month (including four from Uzbekistan), prompting the *New York Times* to declare that NewsBiscuit was Britain's answer to *The Onion*. The website was founded by John O'Farrell (with a bit of help from his former co-writers on *Spitting Image* and *Have I Got News For You* Mark Burton and Pete Sinclair), and combines comedy writing from seasoned professionals with the work of some very talented newcomers who have made their debut on the site.

Apart from entertaining bored people sitting at their office computers, one of the reasons for setting up NewsBiscuit was to provide an outlet for new comedy writers, and in this regard the site has been more successful than any of us dared hope. (Indeed, between them they have originated nearly half of the ideas in this book). In the unlikely event that you're interested, it works like this: NewsBiscuit has an open submissions board where anyone can post a comic story or one-liner, and this material is rated by other fans of the site. The highest-scoring entries are considered for the front page. Other writers on the submissions board are encouraged to suggest extra jokes or alternative punch-lines and a form of 'Wiki-comedy writing' has developed where stories can end up being co-written by several writers in different parts of the world. Some regulars have also teamed up to establish their own virtual writing rooms away from the site in order that they can work together to produce more polished co-written material to NewsBiscuit. Although most stories are usually rewritten by the editor, a majority of front pages now originate on the submissions board. Some of the most successful new writers have gone on to get material on radio shows such as *The Now Show* and *Look Away Now*, as well on the NewsBiscuit radio show that was commissioned by Radio 4 Light Entertainment. Basically, the whole thing is an elaborate scam for John O'Farrell to groom young men on the internet. If you fancy trying your hand at comedy writing, or simply watching how a tentatively suggested one-liner can evolve into a fully fledged comic front page, simply log on to **www.newsbiscuit.com** and follow the instructions to confirm the secret password of your internet savings account.

Special thanks should be given to Rob Dee, who continues to produce the outstanding pictures that accompany the front pages for nothing more than one free NewsBiscuit mug every decade (which isn't saying much considering he designed those as well). Enormous thanks also go to Sarah Whitfield, who is chief website wrangler, administrator and the only person in the office to suggest that perhaps we weren't really the millionth visitor to that website. Thanks also to the site's designer Dominic Hawkin and chief techie Paul Clarke, to the designer of this book Nick Avery, to Phil Lord, Becky Jones and Kate Tolley at Transworld, but most of all to all the readers and writers of NewsBiscuit who have made the site such a hit in its first couple of years. It is to them, and of course to Princess Diana, that this book is dedicated

Isle of Wight to Get Ceefax and other groundbreaking stories from NewsBiscuit was written by John O'Farrell, Mark Burton, Pete Sinclair, Adam Boult, Alex Games, Ant Harrison, Barnabas, Bill Bruce, BudBiscuit, Carl Turner, Chris Cox, David Oliver, Dennis Ringwood, Des Custard, Emma Farrer, Ferrero, Gareth Watkins, Glenn Marshall, Hugh Mothersole, Huwsless, Ian Slatter, James Mylet, James Patching, Jed Madden, Joe Foster, John Annal, John Burns, Jono Parker, Karif, Martin Eggleston aka Zadok, Martin Hallmark, Matt Daniels, Michael Bailey, Neal Doran, Paul 'SuburbanDad' Flowers, Petemc, Phil Philippou, Phil Reed, Phil Smith, Philip Goodfellow, Scott Liddell, Sid of the Suburbs, Smudge, Stephen Ross, Steven Wilson, Stevie Ramone, Team Biscuit (Drew Folland, Ken Roberts, Malc Goring, Matt Vaughan, Rob Dee, Sofie Tayton), Thackaray, The Hit Squad, Toby Smith and Zarguio.